BOOK NEWS

JULIAN MESSNER
Division of Simon & Schuster, Inc.
1 WEST 39th STREET   NEW YORK 10018
TELEPHONE 212-245-6400

Selected Reviews on

MAG WHEELS AND RACING STRIPES
by David J. Abodaher

"...Abodaher discusses the importance of a name and the characteristics of a muscle car and the refinements made because of its use in racing. He tells what a dragster does on the strip, reviews in some detail the 1972 Michigan POR, a 2,000-mile rallye, and touches on swapping engines and restoring old models. He devotes one chapter to sports car magazines and another to the uncertain future of muscle cars because of new federal emission standards. Well illustrated with photographs."
ALA Booklist

"Abodaher's salute to drag racing accelerates faster and f-a-s-t-e-r around the sharp historical bends from the 1910 Austro-Daimler, *the* early sporting model, to the really Super Bearcat of the '30's, on through the 'Mustang revolution' revved up in 1962, to the subsequent 'muscle' car competition which now consumes drivers, fans, rubber, and records alike .... And finally, a squib on the future – the 1975 pollution control standards, the wonderful Wankel, and the adamant prediction that fast, jazzy-looking buggies 'will always be the dream of a big chunk of the American car market.' The theme – beatification of speed and the magical-magnesium wheels that make it happen – will irk those who question the value of auto racing as a sport, please those who would rather hit the go button and dig out."
Kirkus Reviews

MAG WHEELS AND RACING STRIPES

Traces the development of the stock-bodied drag cars from their beginnings in 1910 with the Austro-Daimler and Vauxhall to the present-day Mustangs and Jags. Includes chapters on how car names are chosen, what makes "muscle," trading, drag racing, rallyes, gymkhanas and much more. Exciting reading for muscle car fans.

BOOKS BY DAVID J. ABODAHER

FREEDOM FIGHTER
Casimir Pulaski

MAG WHEELS AND RACING STRIPES

REBEL ON TWO CONTINENTS
Thomas Meagher

WARRIOR ON TWO CONTINENTS
Thaddeus Kosciuszko

Mag Wheels ══════ and Racing Stripes

by DAVID J. ABODAHER

photographs

JULIAN MESSNER   NEW YORK

Published by Julian Messner, a Division of Simon & Schuster, Inc.
1 West 39 Street, New York, N.Y. 10018. All rights reserved.

For my daughter, Lynda

Library of Congress Cataloging in Publication Data

Abodaher, David J
    Mag wheels and racing stripes.

    SUMMARY: Discusses the history, engineering, design, and market-
ing of American sports cars and the various uses of these cars by the
American public.

    1. Sports cars—Juvenile literature. 2. Automobiles, Racing—Juvenile
literature. [1. Sports cars. 2. Automobiles, Racing] I. Title.
TL236.A26   388.34'8'0973   72-1828
ISBN 0-671-32556-6
ISBN 0-671-32557-4 (lib. bdg.)

Printed in the United States of America

ACKNOWLEDGEMENTS

A book of this nature is not written without considerable help from many people. Foremost is the considerate assistance of Tony Weiss of Plymouth and Ed Fleming of Chrysler. Special thanks also must go to Ed Bass of Petersen Publishing, Ken Myers of A. R. Brasch, Inc., Tom Jacobowsky of Dodge, Bruce McDonald at Chevrolet and John Pichurski of American Motors.

To Carolyn Burke at Ford, Jill Rogers at Pontiac, Bernice and Don Thorber and John Crawford of Car Corporation, John Campbell of SCCA and James Bradley of the Detroit Public Library, my gratitude for help in collecting the many photographs so necessary to such a work.

The author would be guilty of a gross injustice if his gratitude was not warmly extended to Jo Ann White, his editor, for her kindness and patience under trying circumstances, and to Mounir Consul for his efforts in digging out information and photographs to complete the book.

CONTENTS

1

THE MODERN ZOOMIE IS BORN

A hard rain swept across the oval at Watkins Glen, New York, on the afternoon of October 7, 1962. Thirty-five thousand car buffs filled the stands under the dreary, dismal sky to see America's top race drivers compete in the annual running of the Watkins Glen Grand Prix.

Few eyes, however, were focused on the track, where car after car whizzed by. Almost all were fixed on a somewhat strange-looking automobile on display in the infield. Despite the driving rain, thousands were milling around the platform on which the prototype of a new idea in cars was being shown to the public for the first time.

It would be eighteen months before this "odd ball from Detroit," as the more conservative writers described it, would be ready for production, but almost everyone who saw the prototype was ready to place an order. America's young, and its young of heart, had been waiting for just such a car—a car that was different, and reflected the action of the '60s.

MAG WHEELS AND RACING STRIPES

And here it was. Low-slung, measuring less than 29 inches from the ground to the top of the hood, with a short rear deck and a long hood that swept forward and dipped down to seemingly eat up almost all of its over-all length of 154 inches, it was an experimental vehicle. It had only a V-4 engine, which was set not in front under the hood, as in most other American cars, or in the rear, as in the popular Volkswagen, but midships, as was typical of many classic European models.

Finally, here it was—young America's dream on wheels. Its name was Mustang.

More precisely, this mock car unveiled at the Watkins Glen GP that wet October afternoon should be identified as experimental Mustang I. In few ways did it resemble the Mustang that would sweep production and sales records off the boards in early 1964 when it was offered for sale. In

Ford Motor Company

First Mustang Prototype

no way was it anything like the typical production vehicle that was then being sold to the American motoring public.

Before Mustang was born, the average automobile seen on American roads was big and bulky, designed for family comfort, and slow, particularly on pickup. There were already Thunderbirds and Corvettes, of course, but such cars were hardly average. And, compared with the standard models made by Ford, General Motors, American Motors and Chrysler, the 'Birds and 'Vets were expensive. The young man going to college, the youth just out of the army and the young recently marrieds could hardly afford them.

To understand why the Ford Motor Company would gamble many millions of dollars producing an experimental car, one must understand the highly competitive nature of the automobile industry. Competition was especially keen between the two giants of the industry, GM and Ford, with Ford playing second fiddle year after year to GM, especially to its Chevrolet Division.

In every business it is axiomatic that you can sell only when you make what the public wants. Every automobile manufacturer, recognizing this fact, maintains a large and highly trained research department that tries to measure, as early as possible, any changes in customer buying habits and desires. The one who hits the market first with that "something different" the motoring public as a whole is waiting for rakes in the sales. As in other businesses, the competitors follow suit as quickly as possible.

By the late 1950s, with the Korean War ended and many thousands of young Americans returning to civilian life, market researchers at both General Motors and Ford sensed the beginning of a change. Young people were beginning to take over, becoming the majority of the purchasers of automobiles. And their tastes were unlike those of the older buyers who had been dictating trends in automobile styling and performance.

Surveys were made. Veterans, college students and young marrieds were polled, as well as older generation drivers. The majority seemed obviously disenchanted with what they were being offered. Other surveys were made. The desire for something "different" was even more pronounced.

What were these "new" buyers looking for? A smaller, easier-to-handle car, for one thing. For another, an automobile that was styled with some zip and pizzazz, lower, longer in front and shorter in the rear deck, like the smart European models with which returning soldiers had become familiar. And they wanted cars that performed with zoom, hot little cars that could go from zero to sixty in seven or eight seconds. A price practical for the young adult was another important consideration.

Very likely it was Lee A. Ioccoca, head man at Ford Motor Company's Ford Division, who first sensed the full significance of the research surveys. Now known to be the genius behind the Mustang revolution, Ioccoca had designers and engineers at their drawing boards before 1960.

It may have been before, it may have been after Ford's move, but almost simultaneously, Chevrolet Division of General Motors started work on what they tentatively considered a smaller version of their highly successful Corvette. At Chevrolet, however, there seemed to be no great rush. The division's experience with the ill-fated Corvair might have resulted in overcautiousness, or Chevrolet might have felt Ford would proceed slowly after its own disaster with the Edsel.

Everything at both Ford and Chevrolet was supposed to

The "new" kind of buyer watching a gymkhana

be totally hush-hush; but the battle lines were drawn. Each wanted to beat the other to the market.

Secrecy is vitally important to every car maker. Tight security on *any* information relative to new models, especially specifications and other details, is a must. Only when it's time to unveil the new, with all the fanfare typical of the automobile business, can the competition—and the buying public—really find out.

Ford was way ahead of Chevrolet in both design and engineering as 1962 approached. Though there were a few variations of the basic car projected for production, Lee Ioccoca held up any final determination, uncertain which of these variables would be incorporated.

During the fall of 1961, Ioccoca visited the Paris Auto Show. There the lines of a specific car caught his eye. The car itself has never been identified, although rumor had it that the car was an Italian design. At any rate, the styling that attracted Ioccoca was, as the story goes, similar to one of the designs being considered at the Ford styling center. Mr. Ioccoca cabled his office with instructions to go full speed ahead. He had made up his mind.

The finished, approved specifications of an automobile—whether in body styling or engineering—are the result of long and tedious labor over a drawing board, followed by multistep operations leading to manufacture. In body styling alone, for example, each component part—hood, door, fender, roof or whatever—is carefully considered by the designer as an element of the total vehicle.

Ordinarily, the first step after basic specifications have been set is the building of a clay model of the car in actual size. The individual body components are then scanned optically to determine the physical dimensions of the part. De-

Lee A. Ioccoca,
Father of Mustang

signers work on these specific dimensions, refining and adjusting until each not only is correct in dimensions but also harmonizes with the over-all body styling.

Once all body components are approved, each is made to actual car size from laminated hard woods, with all the parts finally assembled. The end result is the complete body of the planned car fashioned of wood. If this wood model is approved, production dies are cast from the components.

Ford executives felt that much work remained to be done before the new car would be finalized. Information security or not, however, Detroit was buzzing about the unusual new sports-type car Ford was getting ready. As the automotive writers themselves began speculating in print about a two-passenger Ford called Mustang that would be unveiled during the running of the Grand Prix at Watkins Glen, Ford realized that something had to be done. Not fully aware of what Chevrolet had in mind, Ford would have to move fast to assure that they would be first.

The experimental Mustang I was sent to Watkins Glen in October, 1962, as a smokescreen show car. Its features included just enough of what Mustang would ultimately have to whet the appetite. Within a few minutes of the unveiling, Ford knew they were on the right track. Mustang I, not the famous drivers or the cars that placed in the race, was the hit of the Grand Prix. The American public was indeed ready for a sporty personal car.

Ford, however, was not quite ready for production. The people who had wanted to place orders at Watkins Glen had to be kept interested. The many thousands of car buffs who wrote to Ford headquarters in Dearborn had to be satisfied. The many questions asked were all dodged—carefully, of course, so as not to dampen interest. Ford designers and engineers assigned to Mustang production went into high gear.

The days and months slipped by and speculation continued at high levels, within the industry and among the general public. The automobile grapevine kept spreading rumors about the new car. Since Ford was not yet ready for formal introduction—and something had to be done, another red herring was dragged across the trail.

Cloak-and-dagger affairs in the automobile industry rival anything Sam Spade or Mannix might dream up. When one car manufacturer has a new car in the works, heads can roll if too many details leak out to the competition. Maintaining secrecy is not easy. Detroit newspapermen, for one thing, are trained to sniff out any radical changes. Agents for companies who supply the automobile business with raw materials or specific parts components make the job even tougher.

They like to talk and, though they may be pledged to secrecy, many are not averse to letting information slip while calling on a customer.

Ford, therefore, had a problem. The general public, as well as the industry, had already been exposed to a Mustang version, the one with an aerodynamic front end unveiled at the 1962 Watkins Glen Grand Prix. Since Ford was not yet ready for full scale production something had to be done to maintain the interest generated at Watkins Glen in 1962. The information released could not give specifics about the real Mustang that was being developed; yet it could not simply redescribe Mustang I. There had to be some changes to justify the lapse of time.

A second Mustang prototype was developed. The back and front ends of Mustang I were chopped off. A set of pointed fenders was added to give the new prototype a different look. Recessed headlights with glass covers for smooth air flow were installed. Mustang I, with its air-stream—styled front, had had no headlights.

This hybrid car, partly actual Mustang-to-be and partly pure fantasy, was dubbed Mustang II. It was sent off with typical fanfare to Watkins Glen in 1963, one year after the first false card, Mustang I, had been played. Ford's prime concern was to determine whether the growing youth market would react as enthusiastically as it had the year before.

The answer was clear. With the public alerted by newspapermen beforehand, the crowd was larger than at the 1962 Grand Prix: it was a hungry, appetite-whetted crowd that liked what it saw and made no bones about it. Ford, however, was not ready to make sales, and thousands who were ready to order a Mustang went away disappointed.

The disappointment was only temporary. Lee Ioccoca had

Finish touches to clay model

Ford Motor Company

Ford Motor Company

Mustang II, Second Prototype

been sure from the beginning. Mustang II's reception at Watkins Glen erased any doubts other Ford executives might have had. Orders at the giant manufacturing complex in Dearborn were crisp and to the point. Put production on an all-out, round-the-clock basis. Make Mustang happen.

New automobile models are traditionally introduced in early fall. Ford was not going to wait. A car that generated so much excitement should make its debut without distraction from other models. It should have the spotlight all to itself.

So it was that within six months after false Mustang II stole the show at Watkins Glen even more dramatically than had false Mustang I, what is acknowledged to be the most successful new car introduction since the Model T came about. The real Mustang made its bow on April 13, 1964, in the Ford Pavilion at the New York World's Fair. That date marked the birth of the modern-day zoomies.

Ford Motor Company

Mustang as finally marketed

MAG WHEELS AND RACING STRIPES

Never had the industry seen such an introduction, so widespread an acceptance. For many months to come, production could not keep pace with demand. A new breed of automobile was swinging through American city streets and country highways.

Priced a thousand dollars or more under the average car being sold and making its bow when the American economy was on the rise, this "different" set of wheels sparked a drastic change in the American life-style. Conservatism faded into the wild blue. A low, sleek, roaring beast that could outdrag the next was something you could drive with pride. Give it the hottest engine your money could buy—and the more cubes, the better—and add four-on-the-floor, a tachometer, wide oval tires with raised white letters, bucket seats and one or many racing stripes, and be king of the crowd.

America's young people claimed this new breed for their own, but others also found in Mustang, and in other models that would follow, a symbol of youth. Swingers and sophisticates, whatever their age, tried to outdo college students and high-school seniors. White- and blue-collar workers, male and female and of all ages, the young marrieds and the middle-aged, even grandmothers of seventy and eighty— all proudly maneuvered their flashy wire-wheeled new cars, with their lesser cubic-inch displacement and automatic shift.

The year 1964 was a great one for young America; but that was only the beginning. Mustang would not have the field all to itself. That is not the way of American industry.

2

COMPETITION SLIPS INTO HIGH GEAR

Ford, in effect, had created a new sports car market by taking the long-hood, short-deck, bucket-seat European styling and combining it with a hefty list of American power and comfort features, naming its creation Mustang. Chevrolet, with a somewhat similar type on its designer's drawing boards, was anxious to capture its share of this market, but the wait was long, two years, during which Mustang racked up a phenomenal success record. Its first-year sales of 425,000 alone were an industry record.

Mustang sales soared to 549,436 in 1966, but before the year was up Chevy led a General Motors blitz into the sports car field with two new entries. The first, a 1967 model, was another jazzy, sleek machine that symbolized youth to a young America, called Camaro. It hit the road with a flourish, to take the Ford performance dare.

To a degree, the first Camaro was a copy of Mustang. Beautiful to look at, with lines sufficiently different to distinguish it from Mustang at a quick glance, it still fit the long-hood, short-deck design Mustang had taken from the Europeans. Its top power came from a 5.7-liter engine with 295 braking horsepower. A Camaro plus were standard front disc brakes.

Camaro was introduced as gunning for Mustang's record. While it did put 100,000 units on the road within seven months after its introduction, it was never able to outsell Mustang in any single sales-record period until June, 1970. On the heels of the original Camaro, Chevrolet offered a Camaro SS option. This included a taut, performance suspension, power brakes, a 300 horsepower V-8 engine and wide-oval tires on seven-inch-wide wheels. A Camaro Rally Sport version was next. This carried a special grille with a resilient wraparound frame, separate bumperettes, "RS" emblems, hidden windshield wipers and distinctive parking lights. Finally there was the racy Camaro Z28, a hot performance package with a special 350-cubic-inch, 360-horsepower V-8 engine, beefed-up competition suspension, special 15-inch wheels for white-lettered wide-oval tires, rally stripes, rear-deck spoiler and Z28 emblems.

General Motors wasn't stopping with its Chevrolet Camaro, however. Its Pontiac Division also got into the act in 1966. Pontiac did a simultaneous two-step that year.

First, the sporting qualities of the Pontiac Tempest were emphasized and Grand Prix, GTO and 2-plus-2 models were made available, offering engines of 6.4- and 6.9-liter capacities that developed more than 330 braking horsepower. Then an entirely new Pontiac was introduced, the Pontiac Firebird Sprint. Firebird began with a 3.8-liter overhead cam six-cylinder engine that provided 215 braking horsepower.

Styled similar to Camaro, Firebird was a quick, moderate

The first Camaro

Camaro SS after four years

Pontiac Firebird

Pontiac Firebird TransAm

success. And, like Camaro, Firebird soon also offered up-
graded performance packages with bigger, more powerful
engines and competition extras. One such package, the
TransAm, is considered one of the sharpest sporty models
on the road by young drivers who are totally performance-
oriented.

The car business being so competitive, Ford wasn't about
to sit by and let General Motors take the full credit for a
variety of offerings. The record set by Mustang was too good
to let slip by default. Additional Ford-built sports models
were sent out to pick up additional parts of the youth market.

Ford's Lincoln-Mercury Division opened up with the "Cat"
in 1967, bringing out a moderate luxury-type personal sports
car, Cougar, including a dressed-up version named Cougar
XR-7. The latter, advertised as being "cool" and "hot" and
"wild and elegant," did fairly well in the market, as did a
third "Cat" called the Cougar Eliminator. (In performance
parlance, "eliminator" refers to a drag car that wins by
eliminating competition in its class by setting a lower elapsed
time.)

The "Eliminator" offered the truest muscle of the three
Cougars from the standpoint of both looks and performance.
It boasted front and rear spoilers, twin outside racing mirrors, a blackout grille, an eliminator stripe the full length
of the body and a black action stripe on hood and scoop.
Its base power came from a 351-cubic-inch V-8 with four-
barrel carburetion.

Equipped with either of its two optional power plants, it
was a bomb capable of blowing off the field. The first of
the two was the "Boss 302"—a high-output 302-cubic-incher
that developed 290 horses at 5,800 rpm. It featured a forged
(not cast) crankshaft, mechanical (not hydraulic) valve lifters

and a 780-cubic-feet-per-minute Holley Carburetor. The second power option was Ford's Cobra Jet 428-cubic-incher, with ram-air intake available that pushed 335 horsepower at 5,200 rpm and was also fitted with the four-barrel Holley Carburetor.

All three Cougars offered a wide variety of performance dress-up and power standard equipment and options, including competition suspension and a full range of instruments, including a tachometer. Combined, they made no startling dent in the market.

A year later, in 1968, Mercury Division came up with another multiple-package entry—the Mercury Cyclone. With a GT and Spoiler model added to a basic Cyclone, the sports car lover again had a wide choice in power and equipment.

The most performance-oriented was the Spoiler, with its CJ 429-4V engine and ram-air induction, functional hood scoop and four-speed transmission with Hurst Shifter. On city streets it looked every bit a racer, with bold racing stripes on a hot, competition-color paint, a front antilift spoiler and rear-deck air-foil spoiler. Like Cougar, Cyclone sold, but not in cheer-about numbers.

Until September, 1967, when the 1968 models were introduced to the public, Ford and Chevrolet had the sports car field almost completely to themselves—"almost" only because Chrysler Corporation's Plymouth Barracuda and Dodge Charger had been slightly refined to give them a small, but hardly significant, fraction of the market.

Following the 1968 introduction, the Big Two sports car manufacturers got some worth-while competition and the sports car field became a Big Three. Plymouth got on the boards seriously with a car that a national magazine described as "the ultimate put-on" when it was first announced.

Mercury Cougar

Mercury Cyclone Spoiler

Plymouth Barracuda

This was Road Runner, America's first no-nonsense, high-performance car.

Chrysler's Marketing Research and Sales Development staff had made a survey in early 1967 and decided to enter the performance car race seriously, but with a near complete U-turn as compared with Chevrolet, Ford and Pontiac. They pointed toward a market for a rugged two-door from which almost every touch of gingerbread inside and out was missing, with extra attention given to the literal performance areas, the engine, driveline, suspension and brakes.

The principal buyer of this type of sports car, Chrysler decided, would be the muscle-minded young male in the 18-to-22-year-old group. A careful breakdown of the total performance car market revealed to Chrysler that this young segment was part of the largest buyer group, individuals who basically were ordinary drivers but who had more than just a passing interest in performance.

Road Runner was designed to please them, with solid performance and with good but not gingerbready looks. For power, it was decided that Plymouth's biggest engine would be provided as standard equipment. Every unnecessary bit of trim and ornamentation was eliminated from the design. All in all, the Road Runner was a relatively inexpensive performance machine.

As a result, Road Runner entered the marketplace with a 383-cubic-inch engine building 335 horsepower at 5,200 rpm. An optional choice was Chrysler's hot Hemi, a competition engine with a hemispherically designed combustion chamber. The Hemi had a 426-cubic-inch displacement, developed 425 horsepower at 5,000 rpm and included unique features that assured a "tough" engine. Its crankshaft was forged and nitrite hardened for maximum strength. The main bearings had extra-wide grooves and ran completely around the shells. Another feature, found on few engines today, was the cross-bolting of main bearing caps—bolting both horizontally and vertically to the lower block—to give them maximum rigidity.

With the Hemi, the suspension was necessarily extra—heavy-duty, with bigger torsion bars and an increased spring rate at the wheels to handle the heavier engine. The camshaft was high-performance, the exhaust system dual. The transmission was a four-speed manual, fully synchronized.

Putting it all together, with either the 383 or Hemi engine, Plymouth built a true fun-to-drive, youth-oriented car and offered it at a price—thanks to dumping frills—the 18-to-22-year-olds could afford. Plymouth was convinced that Road Runner was an outstanding muscle machine the young would go for.

They did, in droves—not quite in the huge herds that had swarmed to the early entries by the Big Two, but sufficiently

to let GM and Ford know they had some hot competition. First-year sales hit 45,000—and Chrysler sales and marketing men had thought they'd be happy hitting a 2,500 top!

The reception for Road Runner was so good that Plymouth continued making the personalized package as hot as the individual buyer wanted it. A 440-6–barrel engine was introduced and offered. Then, with some buyers crying for some of the gingerbread left off the Road Runner to keep price down, a decor package was put together. Seventy-five per cent of the buyers ordered it. Thirty-three per cent bought special-performance hood paint and vinyl roof.

Enthusiasm at Plymouth was so great that in 1970 they pulled out all the stops and set up what they named their "Rapid Transit System." A title with good promotion possibilities, the "system" was Plymouth's way of telling the public that it was establishing basic performance requirements

Plymouth Duster

Left: Plymouth Road Runner

for its muscle cars and not merely "offering cars with big
engines, good suspension, great brakes and fat tires."

The essential qualification for a Plymouth product to become part of the "Rapid Transit System" was an elapsed time
within the 14-second range. Their hope was to provide a
car that would fit the wishes of almost every type of performance buff, from the casual driver to the top name race
driver.

Almost every Plymouth line contributed a modified model
to the "system." Road Runner, which inspired the whole idea,
was fitted with an "Air Grabber" that utilized the hood scoops
to draw cool outside air into the carburetor, rather than hot
under-hood air, since cooler air is denser and helps develop
more power.

Plymouth's Barracuda was redesigned to be referred to as
the "Cuda" and offered as the smallest car available with

MAG WHEELS AND RACING STRIPES

One might think the end had been reached, that the muscle car field for American automobile makers had reached the saturation point. Ford, at least, thought otherwise. It may have been Camaro's inroads into Mustang sales. It could have been Road Runner's unexpected success. At any rate, Ford wasn't quite finished. In 1969 it came up with two more Mustang happenings.

Early in the year one Mustang model was given some modifications to make it a drag winner in super stock racing, and named the Mustang Cobra Jet. Equipped with a 428 engine and beefed-up suspension and heavy-duty shocks, it hit the market and gave its young buyers a choice of "Three on the Tree" or "Four on the Floor" as a way to go, on both street and strip.

Later in 1969 came the hottest Mustang of all, the Mach I. This was a top-performance package with the fresh-air Ram

Ford Motor Company

Cobra Jet

Jet V-8 sporting 428 cubes, an engine that would do everything asked of it wherever it was asked. Expensive in comparison with other Mustang machines, it promised the quiet
and comfortable ride of a family car while sporting mean-
looking side scoops and a full spoiler rear.

A casual walk down any major city street, or a visit to
one of the hundreds of drag strips or racing ovals between
the two oceans, will prove what a wide variety of sporty
zoomies have been built. A little experience and you'll be
able to recognize one from the other on sight, for each has
its own individual personality. Most often the very image the
car conveys reflects the personality of the driver.

Muscle and performance are a style, a contemporary
mood. And moods are as different as people.

3

MUSCLE IS
A MANY SPLENDORED THING

It may be Los Angeles, Chicago, New Orleans or Boston—
or any one of a thousand or more small or large cities in
between. It is nighttime, and you pull up in your Mach I at
a stop light. A Road Runner pulls up beside you. You hear
the saucy "Beep! Beep!" and look over.

There's a smile on the face of the driver of the Road Runner, and he cocks his head in greeting, long blond hair
streaming over his eyes. "Like to run that pile?" he asks.

You know what he means. You can hear his hot power
growling like a big wildcat under the Road Runner hood.
You press gently on the accelerator and send back a roar
from the 429 cubes you've got under the Mach I bonnet.
You wait. The light changes and you're both off in a burn
of rubber, each of you anxious to prove you've got the most
muscle, the best take-off.

For some, that's what muscle or performance is all about.
Can a person really say he's got the best machine, whether

36

it's a Camaro, AMX, Charger, Cyclone or whatever? Even on the race track, where the Richard Pettys, A. J. Foyts, Mario Andrettis and the like know what to do and how to do it, under one circumstance one car wins. The next day, under a similar circumstance, another gets the checkered flag. So what does it all prove? What, really, is a performance car?

On the go, a performance machine is one able to pass quickly and safely on the highway or win on the race circuit. It's a car with those qualities of power, suspension, braking and handling that make it a blaster in competitive events or in normal street driving.

In appearance, it's hood scoops that tell you there's more than average muscle inside, wide tires that say traction is there. It's a raised suspension, chromed pipes, hood lock pins and racing stripes. It's bold, big magnesium wheels.

There's an air of ritual in the way a muscle car buff decides what wheels he wants to swing around town on. He's got to start with how much he can afford, of course. It makes a difference, too, what he's planning to do with his car. If it's just to cruise around and impress his friends, that's one thing. Give it the hot looks, and maybe he can get away with just talking cubes under the hood.

But maybe he really wants to *show* them the action. Maybe he's dreaming of some drag strip competition. Then it's a different ball game when it comes to that all-important package under the bonnet.

There are dozens of factors that have to be considered—things like compression ratio, bore and stroke and torque. Under the hood is just the beginning. There are also axles and axle ratios and ring gear diameter. And you can't short-change the suspension, transmission or tires.

MAG WHEELS AND RACING STRIPES

It starts with the engine, however. And it's not just a matter of how many cubes and how high the horsepower. All the elements have to fit together to give the best performance possible. The surprising thing is that even when you've figured it down to such all-important factors as total weight in ratio to horsepower, how quick you can make a quarter mile from a standing start or what distance you can cover in ten seconds, they all seem so close together that it boggles the mind.

The chart on the following page will give you an idea of how close (at least, in numbers) one engine in a specific muscle machine compares with the others offered since Mustang was introduced. The basic engine specifications are those released by the manufacturer for his entry in the field. The performance results have been compiled from records of the National Hot Rod Association and car-buff magazines who keep an eye peeled on this hotter-than-hot business.

Comparison figures, such as shown on the chart, are interesting. Seldom do they indicate what one might believe at first glance. There are other factors one must consider when, for example, quarter-mile elapsed times from a standing start, or the distance covered in a ten-second period, are compared.

In either case the final figure will be affected by whether or not the two vehicles being compared were both equipped with the same type of transmission and/or the same axle ratios. The driver, too, makes a big difference. Hubie Platt, who set all kinds of drag strip records, would most likely leave anyone else biting the dust, even though his competitor was using the same vehicle with identical equipment.

The car freak who'll be all cranked up about getting to sixty in seven seconds will be so supercharged and desperate that the guy in the next zoomie will show him up that he

MUSCLE CAR POWER AND PERFORMANCE COMPARISONS

SPECIFIC PERFORMANCE MODEL	Mustang Mach I	Chevrolet Camaro 396	Pontiac Firebird	Plymouth Road Runner	Dodge Charger	Mercury Cougar	Plymouth 'Cuda 383
ENGINE:							
Displacement	428 cu. in.	396 cu. in.	400 cu. in.	383 cu. in.	426 cu. in.	428 cu. in.	383 cu. in.
Compression Ratio	10.6:1	10.25:1	10.75:1	10.0:1	10.25:1	10.6:1	10.0:1
Bore and Stroke	4.13" x 3.98"	4.09" x 3.76"	4.12" x 3.75"	4.25" x 3.38"	4.25" x 3.75"	4.13" x 3.98"	4.25" x 3.38"
Horsepower @ rpm	335 @ 5,200	325 @ 4,800	330 @ 4,800	335 @ 5,200	425 @ 5,000	335 @ 5,200	330 @ 5,200
Torque (lbs.-ft.) @ rpm	440 @ 3,400	410 @ 3,200	430 @ 3,300	425 @ 3,400	490 @ 4,000	440 @ 3,400	410 @ 3,600
Carburetor, make. # bbls.	Holley 4V	R'chster 4V	R'chster 4V	Carter 4V	Two Carter 4V	Holley 4V	Carter 4V
PERFORMANCE ACTION:							
Standing-to-¼-mile time	13.74 secs.	14.90 secs.	14.21 secs.	14.7 secs.	13.68 secs.	13.90 secs.	14.12 secs.
Distance in 10 secs.	650 ft.	583 ft.	607 ft.	584 ft.	625 ft.	639 ft.	583 ft.
Lbs./Horsepower Index	10.30	9.17	9.48	10.31	8.01	11.02	9.50

fights life to the last rpm he can squeeze. Meaning more to the average buff than this prestige, imagined or otherwise, is to have wheels that look today.

Give him the stripes—a wide one down the middle of the bonnet, flanked by two narrow ones. Let them be where he wants them—perhaps all the way across the back, maybe on the sides. Give him mag wheels to set them off, or maybe just let him choose one or a dozen bits of gingerbread to personalize his pride to suit his own personality.

It matters little to Joe, who just loves cars, whether his wheels are more heavily sprung to handle the stress of superpower, or wider-tired than his friend Bill's. They get together, perhaps at a drive-in, and soon a crowd of six or ten classy wheels are lined up, their drivers talking and comparing with each other.

If the talk becomes a little blistery between any two, they may settle it by heading for a nearby street where there's a good straightaway and little chance of the police bothering them. Or if it's an across-the-board, with everybody disagreeing as to which is the hottest in getting away from a standing start, they'll set a date and time for a test at some spot out in the country.

By the time they meet on some isolated country road, the word has spread. Perhaps ten or fifteen cars are scattered about on the shoulders, and maybe thirty or forty other car freaks frame the deserted asphalt strips. Some are the "haves" with their own zoom-buggies. Others just dream of the day they'll make it themselves.

They line up, as many abreast as the width of the road will take. A yellow Firebird TransAm, its rear spoiler seemingly thumbing at the field, purrs waiting. A black Charger with bright red stripes roars scorn from the depths of its Hemi.

Car Corporation

Typical race-track infield jammed with spectators and cars waiting for the race to start.

MAG WHEELS AND RACING STRIPES

A Cyclone screams back from its 428 cubes. Tense and grim-faced in 'Cudas, Camaros and Mustangs, others wait for the volunteer starter to drop a makeshift flag.

The exercising accelerators waiting for the Go sign have raised enough of a ruckus that a beam of light shows from a window a half mile away. "Get the show on the road," a bystander yells.

The flag drops to a shouting chorus of Go! The wide-open throats of hot engines blast the night, and acrid smells of exhaust and burned rubber pollute the air. The cars seem to catapult down the pavement side by side, inches apart, nose to nose.

The finish line is just yards ahead, with another make-do flag waiting for the winner. Finally one of the rushing, gushing tons of steel draws away by a hood-length. A winner. Today's grudge is settled.

What difference which one made it? If it was the pink Mustang, the yellow Firebird was there last time, and the black Charger the time before. At one time or another every one of them, perhaps, has tasted the glory. And there's sure to be a next time for anyone who might never have blipped the gas pedal as a signal of triumph.

4

THEY'VE MADE THE SCENE
SINCE WAY BACK WHEN

When Mustang broke the automobile market wide open in 1964, it was more a rebirth than the introduction of a totally new concept. Since the early days of the automobile, there has been demand in varying degrees for the personal sports-type car with distinguishing characteristics of performance, design and popularity.

We have, in fact, gone full circle in the terms used to describe this car group, particularly in the promotion and advertising used by the manufacturers. In 1910, the year that saw the emergence of this type of car, they were commonly referred to as "sporting cars." The first to truly deserve such a designation were two entries in that year's annual Prince Henry Tour, a 2,000-mile trial run in Germany.

One was an Austro-Daimler created by Ferdinand Porsche, who would later become internationally famous for his design of the Mercedes-Benz 'S' series and Volkswagen. The Austro-Daimler had an engine with four separately cast cylinders capable of generating speeds of up to 2,300 revolutions per minute or 104.0 braking horsepower. It was one of the first to utilize overhead valves operated by a single overhead camshaft.

The second was a 300-cubic-inch-displacement Vauxhall built in England, developing 60 braking horsepower at 2,800 rpm. Its performance in the 1910 Prince Henry Tour could not approach any of three Austro-Daimlers entered, all of which finished among the first three. Porsche himself had driven the winner.

Prior to that time there were but two types of automobiles, the touring (or passenger) car and the racing car. The Austro-Daimlers and the Vauxhall were considered as rating about midway between the touring models and racing cars of the day and were called "sporting cars" to distinguish their differences in body design and engineering from the other two.

The differences were not great. The "sporting" models incorporated some of the comfort and maneuverability of the touring/passenger cars. They were engineered to give some of the speed for which pure racing cars were built. By the 1920s sporting cars were a big thing, especially in England and on the Continent. The decade of the '20s has been called the Golden Age of Sports Cars.

The Great Depression of 1929, a world-wide financial calamity, brought a temporary halt to the development and manufacture of the sports-type vehicle, because its basic market was limited. A resurgence got under way about 1934, but in most countries all manufacture was stopped when World War II called for the conversion of factories to produce arms materiel.

Following the end of the war, as production was restored, the sports-type car had its first rebirth. Designed and engineered to more closely resemble racing cars, they took on

Early Austro-Daimler

Early Vauxhall

a new name. They became performance cars in the industry. So they were called until Mustang sparked the second rebirth. Because of their high cost, the cars of the sports/performance type marketed prior to Mustang did not have the broad marketability that 1964 was to bring.

With Mustang a new descriptive word for these cars was coined. Now they became referred to as "Muscle Cars" to reflect the increased power and speed. Today, both performance and muscle are soft-pedaled, and we find them referred to, much as they were in 1910, as personal sports cars.

The reason is clear. As the 1970s rolled around and Ralph Nader had made his mark on the American consciousness, a hue and cry was raised for safer driving on American roads. At the same time, emphasis was being laid on the necessity for cleaner air.

The concern over air pollution has brought governmental regulations requiring the installation of emission controls. By their very nature, these controls cut back an engine's power and performance.

Automobile executives are, in the main, a careful and wary lot. With the advertising of power and speed being related to assaults on motherhood or the flag, they have pulled in their promotional horns. The words "muscle" and "performance" have faded from use in radio and television commercials as well as in newspaper and magazine ads. We're back to calling these popular long-hooded and low-slung vehicles "sports cars."

Not that muscle and performance, per se, have totally disappeared. Both are still evident on the racing circuits, and the muscle/performance models—turned—sports cars—whether Ford Mustang, Mercury Cyclone, Chevrolet Camaro, Pontiac TransAm, AMC Javelin or whatever—keep outdoing each other at Riverside, Daytona, Charlotte, Atlanta, Watkins Glen and other points north, south, east and west—not to forget the annual Indianapolis 500 and the European competitions at Le Mans, Monte Carlo, Baden-Baden, Strasbourg and others, where the American cars often run second best to Lancias, Peugots and Ferraris.

At home, on street as well as strip, muscle and performance can be had. If you just can't make it without the thrill of a Gran Tourismo feel, look and action, you can do something about it even if the Camaro, Mustang or Road Runner you buy now doesn't have the flash you want. You can make subtle changes on your own by adding performance parts and accessories to the "personal sports car" you get at your dealer's.

To add the "feel and action" to the sporty one of your choice, there are special camshaft kits, manifolds, carburetors with four barrels, distributors, steel shim head gaskets, valve covers and other muscle-building parts. For the "feel and look" there are special T-bars, jazzy shift knobs, hood-pin kits, mag wheels, fender decals and a multitude of additional look-sharpening items that spell out the driver's own brand of performance.

Not that the average guy or gal who wants to make the scene can just go out and get a sporty car souped up. All vehicles, sports type and otherwise, are now, by federal law, equipped with crank case ventilation, exhaust emission control and fuel evaporation systems. Functionally, these systems are expected to materially reduce the quantity of crank case gases, certain unburned substances and fuel vapors that normally would be discharged into the atmosphere.

Modifications to the original law lay it on the line. If any changes are made in the systems as installed by the manufacturer before the first sale and registration of the vehicle, the buyer and seller are subject to heavy penalties. Some states have passed laws that impose penalties if changes are made after first sale and registration. Then, too, federal law prohibits manufacturers and car dealers from knowingly removing or rendering emission control systems inactive after the sale and delivery of the vehicle. Canadian laws are just as restrictive.

Giving a car a stepped-up performance look is not restricted, however. Those who don't follow the few who soup up at least dress up their Javelins, Road Runners, Barracudas, Mustangs and Camaros to the extent their money lets them.

For call them what you will—sporting cars, performance zombies, muscle machines or personal sports cars—they've been with us since automobiles were first built. As the skeptics of the horseless carriage said in the early days, "in the beginning they were all sporting cars."

The first sporting car built in the United States was most likely the Stanley Steamer. Stanleys had outlasted the many other "steam" cars around the turn of the century, many of which had converted to the internal combustion engine, with others simply ceasing to exist.

In 1906 the Stanley Model H—the "Gentleman's Speedy Roadster"—took to the road with a 23-inch boiler and 20-horsepower engine. A boat-shaped experimental Stanley with an engine rating only 30 hp had just set a new Land Speed Record of 127 miles per hour. When the Model H in its 20-hp version produced for public sale won a 15-mile handicap race at Ormond Beach, Florida, with an average speed of 68.8 mph and recorded 75 mph through a single half hour, it was advertised as the "fastest stock car in the world."

Stanley's pride in his steamer was a legend. The story is

1908 Stanley "Gentleman's Speedy Roadster"

told about F. E. Stanley being hauled into court in Massachusetts and charged with doing sixty near Boston. He pleaded not guilty. The judge, surprised that a man of Stanley's reputation might lie when the evidence was so great against him, asked the auto builder how he could justify his denial of the charge.

"I've pleaded not guilty to 60 miles an hour, your honor," Stanley explained. "When I passed that officer, I saw that my speedometer read 87 miles an hour."

Stanley paid a five-dollar fine, but neither the speed of his "fastest stock cars in the world" nor his pride in their efficiency had any great effect on the buying public. While some Stanley Steamers may still be seen now and then, chugging along on their water "fuel," they were built before 1920. As early as 1912, when Cadillac introduced an electric self-starter, the steamer was on its way out.

Automobiles with internal combustion engines at that time

49

started making more and more headlines. While Stanleys remained in production, their sales decreased drastically as other fine "sporting cars" were hitting the roads powered by gasoline.

Names, most of which are today strange, were the big "sporting thing" in the decade before the 1920s. Apperson, Kissel, Marion, Scripps-Booth, Peerless, Locomobile and Sharp-Arrow were just a few. A "Sportsman" by Maxwell, a name familiar to us today thanks to comedian Jack Benny, was another. There were also Stutz Bearcats and Deusenbergs that in the '20s would be the eye-catchers that Mustang Mach I, Camaro Z28 and Pontiac TransAm became some fifty years later.

The decade of the '20s has been called the Golden Age of Sports Cars. The end of World War I had sparked the first great demand for automobiles with a personality. Busi-

1914 Stutz Bearcat

Detroit Public Library

ness was improving, and money was more plentiful; as before, the initial push began in England and on the Continent. There the great strides made in development of aircraft engines led to automobiles engineered with what was considered unbelievable power.

Prominent among the road-eating monsters were the V-12 Sunbeam with 225 hp, the 275-hp V-12 Rolls Royce Falcon and the 300-hp six-cylinder Maybach. Now and then some well-heeled nabob would have his own built, taking something from this car and something from that. Typical was the original "Chitty-Chitty-Bang-Bang," owned by Count Louis Zborowski, who lived near Canterbury, England.

Count Zborowski had made a convert to sports-type cars in 1890 of the then Prince of Wales. He had maintained his passion for hot machines through the years and in 1913 had provided the financial backing for the English Aston-Martin. His Chitty-Chitty-Bang-Bang had a 23-liter Maybach engine mounted in a chain-driven Mercedes chassis with a Mercedes radiator, gearbox and clutch. It was the forerunner of today's Mercedes-Benz Chitty II.

Bentley, still a magic name among fine sports-type cars, began to be heard from in the early 1920s. In May, 1919, Bentley had announced a new three-liter car, providing an artist's drawing rather than a photograph because the car itself was not yet built. W. O. Bentley had described to Gordon Crosby, an outstanding English artist, his conception of what the car should look like. He told Crosby to use his own imagination.

Crosby must have been an automobile designer at heart. His drawing became the Bentley almost line for line. Though it would take Bentley two years to market his first car, it featured at least two Crosby creations—the Bentley emblem,

51

1929 Bentley

1952 Fiat

1951 Ferrari

1966 MG Midget

1967 Mercedes-Benz exterior

1967 Mercedes-Benz interior

1933 Duesenberg

1951 Porsche

a winged B, and the familiar and famous Bentley radiator. Once on the market, Bentleys stole the headlines. They won Le Mans races in 1924, 1927, 1928, 1929 and 1930.

Other great forerunners of today's sports cars were being manufactured, sold and raced during the '20s in England and across continental Europe. England produced the Vauxhall, MG, Alvis and Atla, among others. The many French cars included Peugot, Citroen, Amilcar, Darracq, Omega and the odd-ball Darmont 3-Wheeler. Germany claimed Mercedes-Benz, Bugatti and Adler-Trumf; Austria, the Austro-Daimler; Denmark, the Opel; Belgium, the Minerva; Spain, the David and Hispano-Suiza; and Italy, the Maserati, Alfa-Romeo, Isotta-Fraschini, O.M. and Ceirano.

The '20s, as a Golden Age for sports cars, went into reverse as far as the United States was concerned. Exciting cars like the Stutz Bearcat and the L-Head Mercer went downhill in popularity. In an attempt at recovery the automobile manufacturers tried the sedate, conventional way. There were, however, a few American speedsters that flashed across the horizon for comparatively brief periods.

One was the Paige Daytona, a sleek speedster that established a stock car record of 102.83 mph in a flying mile at Daytona Beach in 1921, and that same year entered the Pike's Peak climb. The Paige Daytona had a 5.4-liter six-cylinder engine that developed 66 braking horsepower, and a somewhat unusual body. Sporting two seats, it featured a third which could be pulled out from the side like a bureau drawer. For 1923 it added to its sporty dress, being outfitted with front and rear bumpers, spare wheels mounted on each side, a rear-view mirror, clock, cigar lighter and what we would today call an automatic windshield wiper. Windshields were called windscreens in those days (and still are in Britain).

As the '20s began to swing into the '30s, sporting cars had

an American rebirth. Stutz made a dramatic comeback with a Super Bearcat, and such temporarily famous names as Jordan, Auburn, Cunningham, Marmon and Cord had exciting moments in the spotlight.

Beginning in the mid-'30s, sporting-type cars suffered a slow death on the American scene. Comfort and convenience were becoming the big thing, and manufacturers put the accent on economy and closed cars after the Depression left its mark on the economy. The giants of the automobile business were out to beat each other.

Ford, with its Model T, Model A and then Lincoln, had been the sales leader as a result of Henry Ford's determination to put a car within reach of even the blue-collar laborer. General Motors absorbed Chevrolet in 1917 but could not match Ford until the '30s. In third place behind Ford and Dodge, Chevy finally came out with smaller versions of Buick and Oldsmobile and ultimately dislodged Ford in total sales.

The battle continued, and still goes on. Chrysler added to the fire, making off-and-on inroads on the Ford and Chevrolet entries and finally making the automobile giants a Big Three. There were Nashes and Hudsons, both of which later would lose their identity and become the fourth of the major American manufacturers, American Motors.

By 1940 sports cars, as a type, were hardly to be seen except on the race tracks. Ford, Chevrolet and Chrysler built special cars for prestige races such as the Indianapolis 500, and began serious participation in stock car events as well as such overseas tours as the Le Mans and Grand Prix.

The American roads, however, were being traveled by coupes and sedans—sober, solid and substantial types. There were roadsters, of course—an open body style that would evolve into the convertible; but these, the closest to a sporty car, were far in the minority.

5

COMEBACK VIA CORVETTE
AND THUNDERBIRD

When V-J Day brought an end to the U.S. role in World War
II, the last thing an American would have dreamed of was
owning a sports-type car—at least, not a new one, since all
manufacture had switched to war materials more than three
years before. A car buyer could do no more than sign an
order and hope the wait would not be too long.

It was not a short wait, and its length helped develop a
reversal in American automobile tastes. England began turning out new cars before the manufacturers in the United
States could get going. English cars were available for ex-
port. The question was whether or not the trim, sporty British
cars could make it on the western shore of the Atlantic.

The answer was soon obvious. American soldiers had become accustomed to the smaller, sportier English and European cars. And, since all indications pointed to the fact that
postwar American cars would first be carry-over designs from

prewar days, the States could be a profitable selling ground for the European manufacturers.

Exports began in early 1946 with the little MG Midget. Jaguar, which had begun production only the year before, followed. With London and most of southern England badly in need of rebuilding and money scarce in the British Isles, the British not only made exporting as easy as possible but also put on a heavy advertising and merchandising campaign.

The MG Midget was hardly the kind of car Americans would flip over, even though it was considered "cute" in comparison with American cars with their—as one writer put it—gaudy, mouth-organ grilles. It did not have the speed and acceleration that American drivers wanted, a small hill taxed its power and its engine required continuous shifting in traffic. It could be had, however, and its availability overrode everything else.

To help things along, the American economy was at an all-time high. Almost every American could afford a new car —and most needed one. In addition, the ownership of a new car became a big thing for the average citizen. He had become more knowledgeable about automobiles and, as a result, more choosy.

For the first time, too, automobile racing began to mean more to the man in the street than the annual Indianapolis Speedway classic. He began talking about the cars that made it in the European Grand Prix runs and the Le Mans.

It is not surprising that when the Jaguar XK120, a stock car that cost $4,000 or thereabouts, was delivered in the United States, it became an overnight sensation. It could do better than 130 mph, yet it was reliable and economical despite its power. And it had the racy, low-slung looks that

Americans were learning to like and American cars sadly lacked. If one couldn't afford the Jag, there was always the MG Midget, the Fiat or the Triumph.

Soon there was a minor flood of sporty imports from across the ocean. Most weren't to be seen on just any city street, but they made their appearances at country clubs and posh night clubs, proudly wheeled by well-heeled (and some not so well-heeled) Americans. Ferraris and Porsches were among the most popular, along with the Jaguar. But an occasional Veritas Scorpion from Denmark, a Spyder sports Bandini from Italy, or a Pegaso Z-102 from Spain caught a few eyes and turned a few heads.

The important thing was that the eyes of American automobile manufacturers were opened. It was too big a business to let slide across the Atlantic without a fight of some sort. A fight for the business meant a radical change in thinking, so some foreign designers—especially Italians—were brought over. The strong frames and functionally designed bodies of the foreign cars were translated into stronger chassis and more practical body designs in the American.

Designers of American cars began rounding out sharp body corners to minimize wind drag. They scrapped the big, high-off-the-ground styling and lowered the over-all height. They aimed for a car a step or two ahead of the European sports cars that had turned American heads.

General Motors and Ford, almost simultaneously, decided to build an automobile that would be slightly larger and more powerful than the foreign imports. But it would be one that retained, and perhaps improved upon, the low, lean styling of a Jaguar. The one requirement was that it had to be a car that was fun to drive.

GM—or, more precisely, its Chevrolet Division—beat Ford

Comeback Via Corvette and Thunderbird

to the draw by unveiling a "dream car" named Corvette at the 1953 Motorama. Officially introduced in June that year, its most unusual feature was a body constructed of reinforced Fiberglas fitted on a conventional type of frame.

That first Corvette was available only as a soft-top convertible seating just two passengers, the driver plus one, on individual bucket seats. Its styling was attractive and simple in line, proportioned in the long-hood, short-deck fashion of the Europeans. It seemed everything it was created to be, the most striking American sports car since the classic Stutz Bearcat.

Chevrolet, however, was guilty of a major goof. It used the stock six-cylinder Chevrolet engine, a 3.7-liter side-valve power plant. There had been plenty of skeptics when word of the Corvette first leaked out. Car experts were sure it would be little more than another GM spectacular, another

Chevrolet Division GM

First Corvette

pretty-to-look-at job in metal and plastic. In no way could this car-to-be come close to competing with the foreign machines in performance, much less in riding qualities. And here it was, trying to match Jaguar with an ordinary Chevrolet engine!

The experts were not too far wrong for a start. Corvette proved not to have the performance and maneuverability that was hoped for, which may account for its low 300-unit production that first year. Chevrolet was dead serious about Corvette, however. It began a series of tests and changes.

In 1956 it was given a new 4.3-liter overhead valve V-8 engine which produced 189 braking horsepower. It was getting there. By 1969 Corvette developed 290 bhp from a new fuel-injection engine, and the car was so comfortable that it could be driven for hours at high speeds without tiring power plant or driver. It could outcorner any other domestic car. It could leave a Jaguar standing in a drag take-off.

Corvette had truly arrived—young America's dream machine, a true muscle car with a contemporary sleekness and performance that had those who couldn't afford its price drooling with envy. Production in 1969 was a record 38,762, a figure never previously approached by any sports-type vehicle. On November 7, 1969, Corvette could claim the 250,000th car off the Chevrolet assembly line.

The car buying public was astonished at Chevy's audacity in modifying the original Corvette—tripling carburetion, installing a special hot camshaft and going to full-pressure lubrication, aluminum pistons and a dual exhaust instead of the usual single exhaust in stock cars.

So beautiful a car should have maintained the position of those glory days. Corvette tried, but couldn't make it as a star racing machine. While it enjoyed some success in stock car events, an experimental Corvette SS failed at Sebring and, after being entered at Le Mans, was withdrawn from the competition.

Part of the problem in the marketplace was price. Not that Chevrolet Division overpriced the car. The factory-suggested retail delivered price, considerably lower than the cost of a Jaguar, made it a desirable buy. Chevrolet Dealers, however, shot the price sky-high by loading the car with outlandish accessories that added up to near $5,000.

That kind of money could buy a true luxury car, so why— many buyers rationalized—pay that much for a Chevrolet? The true sports car bug had another ache. Corvette had an automatic transmission—GM's torque converter, called Power-glide—and what sports car worthy of the name didn't at least offer four-on-the-floor? At any rate, Corvette sales were on the downgrade.

Ford, as you would expect, wasn't helping the situation. They had, in 1955—two years after Corvette's bow—produced their answering challenge, Thunderbird.

As early as 1949, the Ford Market Research group sensed the growing desire of the American public for an automobile more in keeping with the looks and performance of the Europeans. At the same time, they discovered that the number of families owning two cars was gradually increasing. This two-way potential, combined with the Market Research belief that a freshly styled and engineered car that might appeal to both types of buyers could become a sales blockbuster, got Ford going.

The Ford Product Planning group took its time, carefully assessing the many factors needed to bring the right car to market, because they estimated the market would be ripest in about five years. They planned, from the beginning, with certain specifics in mind.

The projected car would have to be one that could build

Ford Motor Company

First Ford Thunderbird 2-Seater

the Ford reputation on the racing ovals, though that would not be the prime consideration. The number-one aim would be an automobile that could outperform all others in everyday use. It would have to have quicker steering than any then manufactured, exceptional cornering ability and a low, solid but comfortable ride.

As to appearance, this new car could in no way resemble a racer or hot rod. Yet it should have the look of flair with good taste, and should be marketable at a price that would not put it out of reach of middle-class America.

Ford may or may not have been aware of Chevrolet's decision to construct the Corvette body of Fiberglas. They considered it seriously and long but decided against it, partly because of a conviction that automobile buyers were familiar with steel bodies and subconsciously felt them safer. Other decisions included a short wheel base of 102 inches to assure a maneuverable, nimble car; the extra-rigid X-type frame; and equal weight distribution on front and rear wheels.

The latter posed a problem, necessitating the placement of the 4.8-liter V-8 engine with 200 bhp (larger than the Corvette's 4.3-liter, 180-bhp V-8) several inches further back than originally planned. It was planned as a two-seater convertible, but a change in thinking was called for owing to the engine shift. Since there would not be enough room for luggage space plus a well in which to drop a conventional convertible top, they designed a new kind of hard top that could be removed and stored behind the seat back. An innovation of sorts, it made the Thunderbird both a convertible and a closed coupe.

While Ford's Mustang would later beat Chevy's Camaro to market by three years, Ford's Thunderbird, coming out in 1954, was a year late to Chevrolet's Corvette. Significantly, the "Bird" had the same market effect as its little brother, the "Pony," would have ten years later. It swept the boards.

Whereas Corvette showed a total first year production of just 300, some 11,000 Thunderbirds hit the road during its first year. Even after 52 weeks of building T-Birds at a 65-per-day pace, Ford was still two months or more behind in filling orders.

Thunderbird was a car that answered every demand of the most rabid sports car bug, even though it was advertised as a "personal car," not a sports car. It boasted a pounds-per-horsepower acceleration ratio of 14 to 1. It offered a full range of transmissions: automatic, manual synchromesh or overdrive. Its conveniences were as broad as the buyer's pocketbook could make them, providing such options as power steering, power brakes, power seats and power windows. Its basic price was under $2,700.

MAG WHEELS AND RACING STRIPES

With Thunderbird, Ford succeeded in making a sports-type car fit the desires of all kinds of drivers. The young and performance-minded, the older and conservative and almost all between could live with and enjoy this car that was all things to all people. It was, at least for a while.

Through the 1956 and 1957 models, Thunderbird kept its intimate two-seat styling and kept leading the parade. The '57 was an especially sassy job, with a blunt snout and a "fin" back end with twin port-hole exhaust openings jutting out beyond the rear tires like pursed chromed mouths. It was a fiery driving dude—the last of its kind.

For 1958 Ford gave the T-Bird four seats and began downgrading its sports car image. Though it is still produced and holds a high popularity (the millionth Thunderbird came off the line in 1972), it in no way remotely resembles the classics of 1955-57 that still make the eyes pop. Today they are collector's items with price tags of up to $10,000, depending on the model and its condition.

There's no way of telling exactly how many of the 50,504 classic Thunderbirds built between 1955 and 1957 still travel the highways, but the number is considerable. Ford made the change to the four-seater, as one executive explained it, "because it had a larger market, and we had to bypass the loyal T-Bird fans who ride around in berets to get the volume sales."

The loyal fans, even after-the-fact converts, have remained loyal. There was Barbra Streisand, for one, who owned a Bentley in 1965, but ached for one of the T-Bird originals. She looked long and hard and finally landed a '55. Bill Kennedy, former Hollywood actor and now a Detroit television personality, owns a '57 which he bought new. He is still driving it, with the odometer registering near the 120,000-mile mark.

Ford Motor Company

First Thunderbird 4-Seater

"I've had it rebuilt twice," Kennedy says, "and spent $7,000 doing it. But it looks better and runs better than when I bought it."

There are T-Bird fancier clubs throughout the United States. Some 3,500 belong to the San Francisco—based Classic Thunderbird Club International, with chapters in most major metropolitan areas.

They still call the four-seater Bird a "personal" car. Its sales kept rising so that when 85,000-per-year production was nearing in 1965, General Motors—to keep pace and get its share of the personal car market—came out with the Buick Riviera and Olds Toronado challenge.

The conversion of Thunderbird to the four-seater model had, however, put another temporary end to the widespread craze for a truly sporting-type car—a craze Ford revived with Mustang.

6

WHAT'S IN A NAME?

Automobile manufacturers, especially the American breed, firmly believe there's plenty in the name they tag on their creation. As a result, months, sometimes even years, are spent selecting, discarding, deciding, changing minds and starting all over again to find just the right name. Often the machine will be set, ready for the market and still not be dubbed with the exciting, mind-boggling identification the manufacturer wants.

Once the decision is made, the excitement begins, always with the fingers crossed. Even the wisest aren't sure of their choice. Time has proved again and again that a potential car name can't be depended on in advance to hit the buyers' fancy until the public has rolled it around on its collective tongue.

Names must say something. They must tell the buyer something he wants to hear. Big show cars must carry names that suggest the posh, the elegant, the jet set. So we have El

Dorado, Continental, Imperial and Riviera, to name a few. Each says something that hits the prestige-conscious car buyer square in his ego.

There may be nothing to it, but there's a thought or two in automotive circles that a few cars no longer on the scene wound up on the discard pile because their names did them in. Take DeSoto. What did the Spanish explorer who discovered the Mississippi have to do with what a car looked or drove like. The same might be said for Hudson, Edsel, Willys, Packard and a bushel or more of others. Yet General Motors, which had to bury one named for the French explorer La Salle, has lived and made it big with Cadillac, named for another French explorer. So who really knows?

This automobile "name game" is a tough one to play. It is dangerous and complex, and certainly can be very costly if a mistake is made or delays are encountered in getting approval. At one time, as late as 1954, duplications were common and often resulted in wasted advertising dollars and waits of even more than a full year before an appropriate choice was cleared.

No such problems have existed since the Automobile Manufacturers Association organized its Patent Department in 1955. That department today has over 65,000 names on record in its trademark section, names that car companies are now using, intend to use or already have used. In addition, there is a "Proposed Use List" that is held at about 400 names registered annually by the auto makers for possible use. The "Proposeds" are so secret that only the department head and his assistant have access to the list. The association will reveal to a qualified person whether or not a certain name is on file, but will never tell which company is considering use of the name.

MAG WHEELS AND RACING STRIPES

To register a name with the AMA, an official of the car manufacturer or its advertising agency forwards a request to the Patent Department of the AMA. If the name is not registered—and the AMA can usually check its files in 15 minutes or so—the one requesting is notified and the name is placed on the Proposed List. If the name is already listed, the company is told so, but never told to whom it is registered.

Each year the Proposed List is reviewed and the AMA may, at its option, remove a name from the list if the requesting company has not used it within a two-year period and another company is serious about its use. In earlier years names were quickly given to new cars, very often those of the designer or maker. Today it's a serious, careful business.

In no automobile category has the name proved more important than in the muscle and performance field. Often the name has had as much to do with the success of a given machine as what the car offered. In power, looks and whatever it takes to sell, there's not that much to choose between them.

Muscle/performance machines are GO automobiles. The names they bear suggest power, speed, action and even a "watch-out-I'm-dangerous" connotation—the names, that is, of all the popular muscle machines except Camaro. With the unexciting idea of implying a friendship between owner and car, Chevrolet converted the French word for pal or comrade, *camaro.*

Mustang, as the first of the modern-day sports type, became Mustang through an interesting string of circumstances that speaks volumes for the way automobile makers agonize over the names they give their cars and the effect the names may have on the public. No one at Ford will admit to the truth of the story—at least, not in public—but the tale has gone the rounds since before Mustang's official introduction.

It seems that Torino was the name first selected for this new machine designed to appeal to the youth crowd. The decision was made, it is said, about the same time that Henry Ford II, recently divorced, was spending so much time in Europe courting the charming and lovely Italian to whom he is now married. Someone at Ford became fear-stricken that unfavorable implications might result from giving their new car an Italian name at that time.

Whether the story is true or not, it was thumbs down on Torino. Next came the decision to call the car Cougar. Somehow, it was felt, the name Cougar would give the car the wrong image. Mustang was actually a third choice, and what a decision that was. No name before or since so completely captured the young car buyer's imagination.

Cougar and Torino, of course, didn't die as names. Ford's Lincoln-Mercury Division came out later with a sporty personal car they called Cougar. And after Mr. Ford's marriage to the now Christina Ford, a Ford Division car was tabbed Torino.

Cougar, and the way it is advertised, is typical of the spirit behind naming the majority of muscle cars. It is named for a predatory animal from the cat family, the sleek and slinky animal that is second only to the jaguar in ferociousness among American cats. Ford uses a live Cougar and its vicious growl as the "Cat's" (as the car is called) trademark. Jaguar, of course, was the name given a fine English sports car as far back as 1945.

Among the other muscle machines, Dodge Charger suggests a war horse. Mercury's Cyclone conjures up visions of a violent windstorm sweeping across the highway. Hear the

Cobra Insignia

name Cobra and you imagine quick, darting fangs hissing a venomous jet stream. Barracuda reminds one of the huge, deadly fish found in the Caribbean. Corvette means a warship.

Thunderbird was originally going to be called Fairlane after the luxurious and gracious estate of the first Henry Ford in Dearborn, Michigan. The name Fairlane, however, could have appealed to the prestige-conscious and hardly reflected the dramatic styling of the car's design and what it was meant to do on the road.

A Ford designer named Alden Giberson had lived in New Mexico while working on the Los Alamos atomic energy project. He had seen, and had been fascinated by, the savage-looking symbol the Indians called Thunderbird, and suggested it as a possible name and trademark. It was beautiful and simple. Such other potential names as El Tigre and

Thunderbird Insignia

Coronado were quickly discarded, and Thunderbird was born.

A bird of another name, Firebird, was also called after a legendary Indian symbol. This, from the north country, promised action, youth, power and beauty. The description aptly fits their spirited muscle car, the people at Pontiac Division of General Motors will tell you.

Mustang, of course, refers to the speedy, half-wild, hard-to-catch pony of the western American plains. When Ford decided to add a higher-performance Mustang to the model line, the name chosen gave Mustang another aura of matchless speed. They named this Mustang "Mach I" after Ernst Mach, the Austrian scientist and astronomer whose name is synonymous with the breaking of the sound barrier.

Descriptive words or phrases used to identify cars within a model line, such as Mach I or Cobra for Mustang, almost always have special meaning. Eliminator, as used by Cougar, means a drag car that has defeated its field by eliminating other cars in its class by running at a higher speed. GT, a name used by many car makers, is an abbreviation for Gran Turismo, a European-type race car, and usually indicates a two-seater.

If anyone may be considered more fortunate than Ford in selecting Mustang for a name, it would be Chrysler's Plymouth Division in naming their Road Runner. Chrysler Plymouth executives had considered and rejected dozens of names they felt would fit this new entry which was designed to appeal to a youth market interested more in what their machine would do than in what glamour it exhibited.

Plymouth brass had considered the name off and on for two years, but somehow Road Runner had not caught on. Now the executives were in a bind as to what to call their new road machine. One Saturday morning, when the big-wigs were really up-tight trying to make a "name" decision, two product planners, Jack Smith and Gordon Cherry, suggested to J. M. Sturm that he go home and watch a certain Warner Brothers cartoon feature on television.

Sturm, almost reluctantly, tuned in the TV station. In just a few moments he was completely intrigued by the saucy little bird Warner Brothers called Road Runner. He was equally hooked by the catchy "Beep! Beep!" Sturm already knew that young people from coast to coast were echoing that "Beep! Beep!"

Smith and Cherry had hit the jackpot with their suggestion, but Sturm was not too hopeful. It was hardly likely that some business or product had not already tied up use of the name—the promotional possibilities were that great.

Halfheartedly, Sturm went into a staff meeting on Monday morning. He tossed his reaction to the group and suggested that, while he was sure that such a hot property was no longer available, it wouldn't hurt to check with the Automobile Manufacturers Association. The check was made and, hallelujah!, Plymouth could reserve Road Runner as the possible name for its youth-oriented muscle machine!

That was the beginning. Plymouth proceeded to develop a bird character to symbolize the car. No treatment of the bird satisfied. None came close to the daring, saucy Warner Brothers' beep-beeping Road Runner. To get permission for use of the original was worth a try.

Came another, and a double-barreled, surprise. Warner Brothers not only agreed to Plymouth's use of its copyrighted character as a trademark but also tossed the sound track of a Road Runner cartoon into the package.

Plymouth sent the sound track to one of its horn manufac-

Chrysler-Plymouth

Road Runner in Racing Dress

turers. The result was an automobile horn that sent out a "Beep! Beep!" so much like that of the kooky bird seen on theater and television screens that only a trained technician could tell them apart.

Plymouth played the promotional possibilities to the hilt. The sharp, shrill "Beep! Beep!" not only sped across the land from the hoods of new Road Runner automobiles but also was echoed from the throats of the young and not-so-young.

Boys, girls, teen-agers—even gray-haired fathers—went into Plymouth showrooms asking to see the horn. Their puzzled looks and obvious disappointment at seeing nothing more than a black, unadorned, automobile horn stopped them for seconds. Almost always they'd finally smile, give a "Beep! Beep!" of their own and exit.

To offset the disappointment, Plymouth did the next best thing. They had the horn painted purple and affixed to it a decal that read: "Voice of Road Runner." Now, when someone asked to see the horn, they were shown something that at least backed up the car's personality.

The decals themselves became a collector's item. Everybody wanted a reproduction of the audacious cartoon bird. Firebirds, Camaros and Mustangs were seen rolling the streets sporting a Road Runner decal. Some of the competitive cars were even heard beeping with the Road Runner voice.

7

WHAT MAKES MUSCLE?

Muscle, so far as automobiles are concerned, comes from the engine. Much has been made in previous chapters of engine power, cubic inch displacement, compression ratio and other elements which add up to muscle or performance. It may not be off base at this point, especially for readers who may not be fully familiar with the workings of an engine, to review those factors that influence the car maker in designating a specific engine for a particular model and to look at how power is developed in the engine.

All automobile manufacturers plan their engine production facilities to give their customers a choice in the selection of the power plant they prefer for the car they are buying. It is here where such words as "standard engine" or "optional engine" have meaning.

The "standard" engine is the power plant provided for the basic car at no extra cost to the purchaser. What will be set as the "standard" engine comes about through the combined efforts of people in marketing, engineering and manufacturing in the automobile company. They decide what will sell best to the buyer most likely interested in the specific model. The engine that will create the greatest demand at the lowest over-all price for the car is usually designated as "standard." Then other, more powerful engines are offered as "options" which can be substituted for the "standard" at a set increase in cost.

As an example, say you're in the market for a certain sporty car and you want some muscle. The standard engine for your choice has 290 cubic inches of displacement, but you want a more powerful engine. An engine with 383-cubic-inch displacement, which will substantially increase the performance potential of your car is available. This larger engine is an "option," an engine you can have installed in preference to the "standard" if you don't mind paying an additional $300 or more. Both engines have two-barrel carburetion. Designations for the engines are 290-2V or 383-2V, the 2V representing the two-barrel carburetion.

To get an even higher performance kick, you may prefer a four-barrel carburetor, also an option at additional cost. You then wind up with a 383-4V engine. Carrying your desires further, you ask for a D.S.O. (a Dealer Special Order). With a D.S.O. the factory makes up your car special, installing such extra features you may have chosen—perhaps mechanical instead of hydraulic valve lifters and a special camshaft. The latter are also options and build up your total cost.

The fact that a "high-performance look" turns on many dyed-in-the-wool muscle car buffs has already been mentioned. A substantial number are even more interested in the "look" than in raw muscle—especially these days, when performance is being soft-pedaled and more and more women are getting into the act and driving with the "now" image. Special packages that dress up small cars to give them a muscle look are now offered by some car makers. These produce what the industry is calling "cosmetic cars."

But let's say you want that performance look in addition to the muscle. Under the hood you can add chrome components, such as valve covers and air cleaners, that make the engine gleam when the hood is raised. For the exterior you might add hood scoops, spoilers, mag or chrome wheels and special hot, competition paints and/or decorative decals.

Stripes are big, too, and getting bigger. Racing stripes have made the scene for a number of years, but now, with the clamp-down on raw muscle, striping is in greater demand than ever. Increasing this increased demand are new developments outdating the old system, as old as the automobile industry itself, which called for the services of a striping expert, a unique kind of design artisan who could add a straight-as-an-arrow stripe to the body of a car. Painting on a stripe is no longer the thing. Today the machine can be trimmed with a tape-type stripe, premade and applied to body metal.

This new technique, utilizing a vinyl applique bonded to the body with a tight-locking adhesive, is less costly than the painted-on stripe. One new offering, called a laser stripe, comes in reflectorized rainbow hues that shine brightly night and day. It is estimated that at least 50,000 1972 model cars will sport this laser stripe before the model year ends. Further estimates indicate that at least one million 1973 American cars will carry tape stripes.

Regardless of whether he has tape stripes, hood scoops, spoilers or other external muscle looks, the real muscle buff is more interested in the functional performance parts. With or without the "image," he wants what steps up power, control and handling of the car. These can include reinforced suspensions, beefed-up transmissions, such as a four-speed with Hurst Shifter, and special rear-axle ratios.

So you're a genuine muscle machine freak, and you've got the car and the equipment that fits you to a tee. You also have the engine that will deliver power to blast others off the road. So let's get to the specifics of how that power, that muscle, develops.

Air and gasoline make up the only energy fed into an internal combustion engine, however large or small it may be. The amount of energy that can be developed by the engine is determined primarily by how efficiently the fuel and air are used. This available engine power is affected by such elements as piston displacement, compression ratio, in-

For a muscle-car buff, as are these participants in a gymkhana, the car must have performance as well as good looks.

take system pressure, valve and spark timing, engine friction, the ratio of air to fuel, the ability of the engine to withstand speed and pressures and such atmospheric conditions as air temperature, pressure and moisture content.

The volume, or amount, of the air-fuel mixture consumed by the engine is always the same at a particular speed, because the volume is determined and fixed by the engine cylinder volume. The weight of the air-fuel mixture can vary, however, since gases and their mixtures are compressible and weight variations are possible within the same volume.

The engine must *work* to create energy from the gas-air mixture. This energy is the *power* that moves the vehicle. Work is measured in foot-pounds, multiplying distance times force. Power is the rate or speed at which work is accomplished.

To express it simply, the work to make power is done in four stages in each of the cylinders of an engine. The cylinder, open at one end, is fitted closely with a piston which drives a crankshaft by means of a connecting rod. The air-gas mixture is drawn into the cylinder on the first, or intake, stroke. The air-gas mixture is compressed when the piston is moved upward, the second stroke or stage. In the third stage, a timed spark in the upper part of the cylinder ignites the vapor (fuel-gas mixture) and adds heat to the air. By the time the piston has reached the top of the cylinder, the ignited gases are compressing, pushing in all directions. The fourth stage results. The downward force being applied to the top surface of the piston forces it to move in the direction of least resistance, which is down.

From this fourth stage we get the final action. Its force is transferred through the piston pin to the connecting rod and from there to the crankshaft. When the crankshaft rotates, work is being done. How much power that work will generate depends on how fast the work is being done. This is called torque, the amount of turning power exerted by the crank-shaft. It is expressed in pounds-foot (lbs.-ft.) and, when trans-lated into the full power generated by a specific engine, as pounds per foot at so many revolutions per minute (torque at rpm).

How great this power will be is influenced by the cubic inch displacement in the cylinders and the ratio of compres-sion by the piston, the measurement of the bore and stroke of the piston rod, how fast the carburetor feeds fuel and the speed at which air is taken in to be mixed with the fuel in the right proportions for the engine. The end result is the torque-at-rpm figure, finally used to determine the horse-power (actual energy) created. Since it starts with the cubic inch displacement, simple mathematics indicate that

Hubert Platt, famous drag racer, conducts a sports car club seminar on engine performance.

the greater the number of cylinders, the more cubic inch displacement there is. Eight cylinders, for the muscle enthusiast, is obviously to be preferred to six.

Obviously, too, the larger the engine, the more expensive it will be to produce—and the more it will cost you.

The higher price, however, could put the price of the finished car too far out of reach for the greatest number who might be interested. At that point it would be impractical for the car manufacturer to make it, much less offer it for sale.

To understand exactly how this business of supply and demand works in the automobile business, let's take a closer look at the way in which Chrysler Corporation and its Plymouth Division decided on Road Runner. The first step was to find out how extensive the market was for a performance car and how this market for a performance/muscle type machine would break down as to type of buyer.

Since the planning, designing, creating prototypes as sample models, making dies from which body components are formed and all the other details that must be covered in producing the final automobile represent an investment that runs into millions of dollars, the manufacturer has to be fairly sure what type of car to decide on and how great the demand would be for that particular type—which is one of the more important reasons large marketing staffs are employed.

After working carefully and long, Chrysler's marketing group developed a sort of pyramid showing individual groups of potential buyers of a car that was performance oriented.

The smallest group of potential car buyers with interest in performance was represented by the peak of the pyramid, the professional racers and those who make their living on the racing circuits. The group is a small one, but is one that exerts the greatest degree of influence on the entire market.

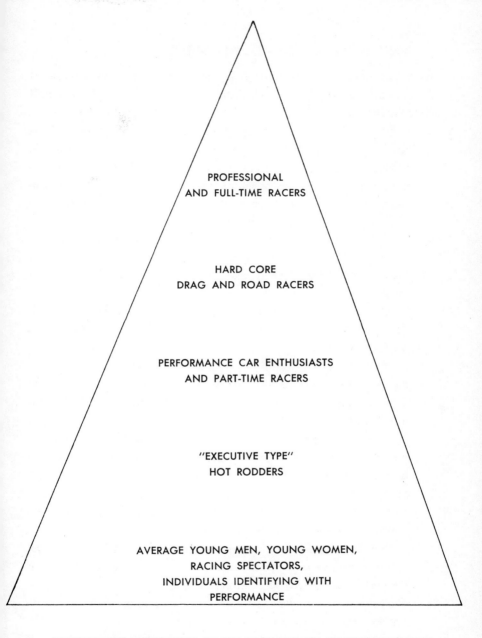

PROFESSIONAL
AND FULL-TIME RACERS

HARD CORE
DRAG AND ROAD RACERS

PERFORMANCE CAR ENTHUSIASTS
AND PART-TIME RACERS

"EXECUTIVE TYPE"
HOT RODDERS

AVERAGE YOUNG MEN, YOUNG WOMEN,
RACING SPECTATORS,
INDIVIDUALS IDENTIFYING WITH
PERFORMANCE

CHRYSLER SIZE BREAKDOWN OF THE PERFORMANCE ENTHUSIAST MARKET

MAG WHEELS AND RACING STRIPES

While their opinions about a car, and their possible use of it, can greatly help in building sales, an automobile built specifically for them would have the most limited market.

The next-smallest group, the hard-core drag and road racers, is also limited in numbers. Chrysler decided that, while they are purists in terms of what they want in and on a car, they represented too small a market. To this group actual performance was far more important than the appearance and reputation of the vehicle.

Next down the pyramid was the part-time racer and individual who was totally gung-ho on muscle. He still demands top performance, but is also particular as to how the car looks.

Chrysler called the next group "executive-type" hot rodders, for want of a better name. This buyer wants good solid performance (not quite as total as the part-time racer), but he is even more particular about a car that looks smooth and expensive. He would be more interested in a "slick" car than in a "tough" one. He would be more apt to buy a fully outfitted Corvette.

The last, and by far the largest, market segment was made up of the average man or woman who had more than just a little interest in performance and would prefer an automobile that could do things and had a not-too-expensive starting price, but could be dressed up to the extent his personal tastes and pocketbook permitted.

This largest buying group, in common with each of the smaller buying segments in the performance car market, did not look on a car as simply a means of transportation. Chrysler decided that *this* was the group to go after—people on the young side and who feel young, who greatly enjoy owning and driving cars for the fun and pleasure of it, the

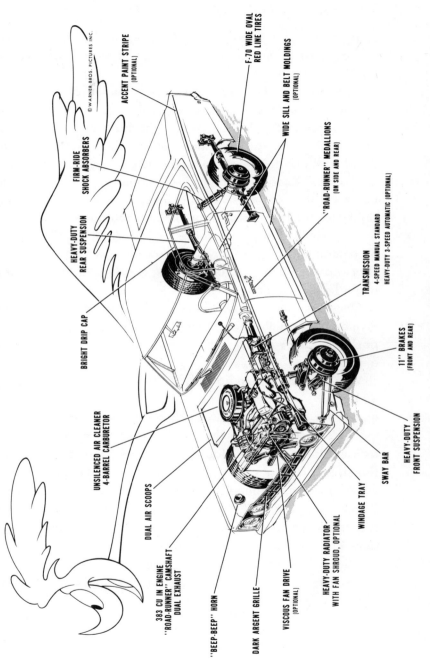

ACCENT PAINT STRIPE
(OPTIONAL)

F-70 WIDE OVAL
RED LINE TIRES

WIDE SILL AND BELT MOLDINGS
(OPTIONAL)

FIRM-RIDE
SHOCK ABSORBERS

"ROAD-RUNNER" MEDALLIONS
(ON SIDE AND REAR)

HEAVY-DUTY
REAR SUSPENSION

TRANSMISSION
4-SPEED MANUAL STANDARD
HEAVY-DUTY 3-SPEED AUTOMATIC (OPTIONAL)

BRIGHT DRIP CAP

11" BRAKES
(FRONT AND REAR)

HEAVY-DUTY
FRONT SUSPENSION

SWAY BAR

WINDAGE TRAY

UNSILENCED AIR CLEANER
4-BARREL CARBURETOR

DUAL AIR SCOOPS

383 CU IN ENGINE
"ROAD-RUNNER" CAMSHAFT
DUAL EXHAUST

"BEEP-BEEP" HORN

DARK ARGENT GRILLE

VISCOUS FAN DRIVE

HEAVY-DUTY RADIATOR
WITH FAN SHROUD, OPTIONAL

©WARNER BROS. PICTURES INC.

Plymouth Road Runner

kind of car buff who nurses and protects his "baby" and spends most of nonwork time fixing, cleaning and driving the car.

Obviously, if Plymouth Division was to sell a lot of cars, the automobile would have to be planned to fit into the needs and desires of this largest group, the base of the pyramid. Starting there, it was more than possible that additional sales could be made to the other segments going up on the pyramid scale. "Executive hot rodders" perhaps not too much, but if the basic car they would call Road Runner was planned right, the hard-core professional racer could use it as a start for a personalized performance vehicle. And, by offering an automobile that was relatively inexpensive, with a sufficiently "hot" base engine, appropriate suspension and brakes, they might have it made.

Once the decision was confirmed, it became the job of Plymouth's own Product Planning group to put together a package that would meet the requirements of the market aimed at.

We've already seen how Plymouth went to their available 383 engine with four-barrel carburetion as the "standard" engine for Road Runner. An optional choice was the blistering 426 Hemi. Keeping the youth market foremost in mind, transmission would be "four-on-the-floor" standard. Suspension and braking systems compatible with the power that would give the handling characteristics that would keep Road Runner "fun to drive" came next—heavy-duty front and rear suspension, heavy-duty shock absorbers, antisway bar, heavy-duty 11-inch brakes and wide oval tires.

With a low, racy body, attractive but not gingerbready, but which could be personalized as the buyer wished, the rest became history.

8

PRO MUSCLE ON STRIP AND OVAL

It was early February, 1967. Ace drivers Ronnie Bucknum and Jerry Titus were piloting Mustangs entered along with a dozen others in the over-two-liter Trans-Am sedan competition at Daytona. Bucknum and Titus were racing the colors of Carroll Shelby, a California car buff who then had close ties with Ford. Listening to the unceasing buzz in the stands, you'd have believed only one other car was on the grounds.

The big to-do that had the crowd heated up was Camaro's chance to down Mustang. No other car, or any other factor in the annual race, seemed to matter. As it turned out, Shelby's Mustangs "blew the doors off all the others" (as one racing writer phrased it) and went on not only to win the checkered flag in their class but also to place fourth over all behind three Porsche 907s. Camaro had bitten the dust.

Pride is almost everything on the racing circuit. A Camaro driver has to believe in the wheels under him, just as the Mustang driver, or the Plymouth or AMC pilot. So Camaro

Mustang at Daytona Beach

wasn't about to take the defeat without a challenge for next time.

"Just you wait, baby!" came the taunt. "Next year Camaro will blow Ford right out of the ballpark!"

It takes luck and a lot more, however, to make good a dare on the racing circuits. Nineteen sixty-eight rolled around at Daytona, and Mustang finished more than 60 laps ahead of Camaro. It was a hollow victory. Camaro had spent over two hours in the pits getting some major engine work done. If there was any satisfaction for the Chevy crew, it had to come from the front suspension that had forced out the second Mustang in the competition.

Rivalry on the stock car circuits is blistering hot. Usually one car wins, then another and perhaps a third in three successive races. Yearlong stock car competition during 1971 is a case in point.

In the Riverside 500, Ray Elder won with a Dodge. On a 125-mile run at Daytona, David Pearson took one event with a Mercury, while another was won by Pete Hamilton in a Plymouth. A 400-mile race at Daytona went to Charley Glotzbach in a Chevrolet, and the Rockingham 500 belonged to Bobby Allison in a Ford.

Forty-seven events for stock cars were run in 1971 under the auspices of the National Association for Stock Car Auto Racing (NASCAR), the world's largest stock car race sanctioning body. Twenty races were won by Plymouth, twelve by Mercury, eight by Dodge, four by Chevrolet and three by Ford. The events ranged from the short 46-miler at Islip, New York, won by Richard Petty in a Plymouth, to the lone 600-miler at Charlotte, North Carolina, where a Mercury swept across the finish with Bobby Allison at the wheel.

Chrysler-Plymouth

Richard Petty and Winning Plymouth

MAG WHEELS AND RACING STRIPES

With twenty wins during the competition year to only twelve for the next best, you might think Richard Petty's victory in the 1971 NASCAR Grand National made Plymouth number one, and the devil take the rest. But consider the seven-year record since the new breed of sports cars came on the scene in 1965. During that seven-year span Plymouth won a total of three National Championships, all wheeled by Richard Petty. Ford, however, also took three and Dodge one. Did that put Ford on a par with Plymouth? It isn't necessarily so. Wins are good to have and good for the ego, but they're not the end-all for the automobile manufacturers.

For one thing, now and then Ford and Chevrolet have pulled out of officially factory-sponsored racing. Cars made by them ran in races regardless, but under personal sponsorship. For the manufacturers, the race track serves primarily as another research facility and victories build glamour and headlines.

Obviously, new ideas are not tried out from scratch on the racetrack. That might prove tragically dangerous. However, a new car that has already been proved practical on the test tracks owned and run by the manufacturers themselves may show the need for adjustment or refinement that improves their value and use. It may also be that parts related to driving, not made by the car manufacturers but purchased by them for installation on their automobiles, do so well in racing competition that they are bought for use on a Ford or Chevrolet or Plymouth instead of one they may be currently using.

Tires are one example. The major tire manufacturers battle to get their tires used by the biggest-name race drivers—especially those who take part in the grueling Indianapolis 500. Tires that can weather the storm at Indy really make it with the car makers as well as the public. The same holds true for pistons, bearings and a host of other car components that are used by the car manufacturers on their automobiles or are independently sold through dealers as replacements.

Disc brakes, for example, common today but hardly known before 1952, came into use as a direct result of racing. Derived from aircraft brakes, they were first used on the 1952 Jaguar in racing at Le Mans. The Jaguar drivers were able to delay braking almost until the last second, as much as 300 yards nearer a hairpin turn, and as a result whipped the field.

Race action has also contributed significantly in refinements that have helped increase the power output of engines. One car may be fitted with pistons and connecting rods lighter in weight than usual, or another with larger valves, and both show appreciable boosts in power.

This is not to say that automobile racing has made any phenomenal contributions to the development of the car, contributions that might not have been made otherwise. Certainly the same refinements, the same improvements, would have come sometime, engineering being what it is. Cars did begin including rear-view mirrors after one was first used in the 1911 Indianapolis 500 by the famous driver Ray Harroun. So simple and useful an addition would certainly have made its appearance on stock cars sooner or later, whether or not it was introduced at Indy.

Competitive professional racing on both the oval and the drag strip benefits both the automotive industry and the driving public. Its greatest and most significant contributions have come, however, not from races won or from top speed records set—or from any standards set for the engineering or body designs of the cars, including muscle and performance ma-

chines. The most worth-while benefits have come in sec-
ondary ways.

Spark plugs, shocks, lubricants and fuels, as well as engine
components including bearings, piston rings and gears—all
of which play a vital role in efficient, economical operation—
are tested in racing cars. After the race is run, these parts
are removed and examined. The result is a constant up-
grading of these elements, with the best quickly picked up
by the industry for use in the cars offered to the public.

However the automobile manufacturers may feel about it,
competitive racing will continue with or without their participation. It is big business and a way of life for the Indy
stars, such as A. J. Foyt, Mario Andretti, the Unsers and the
rest; for the stock car superdrivers like Richard Petty and
Bobby Allison; and for the drag experts, such as Hubie Platt.

As long as companies refine gasoline and oil and build
spark plugs, shock absorbers and engine components, the
great drivers of the racing world will find plenty of sponsors,
all hopeful that a big win here and there will give them meat
for promotions that will sell more gasoline, spark plugs and
whatever. The drivers make money from these promotions,
but the big thrill for them is the winning, the crossing of the
finish line first, when another and bigger pot of gold is
waiting.

This side of automobile racing is definitely big business.
One look at the $100,000-plus purse for the annual India-
napolis 500 tells you that. Because professional racing is
international in scope and (owing to the wide differences
and variations in cars and engines) a complex, confusing
activity, it is supervised and controlled by the Fédération
Internationale de l'Automobile. The FIA is a voluntary band-

Oval Action

In Group 9 are all single-seaters that do not fit a specific formula. This class, dubbed Formula Libre Racing Cars, also has no minimum production.

These classifications were established by the world-wide FIA group. In the United States most road racing competitions are conducted under sanction of the American segment of the FIA, the Sports Car Club of America. The biggest races, such as the Indy 500, also carry full FIA sanction to permit the great drivers from around the world to take part.

Automobiles that race in the high-speed, endurance events, such as the Indianapolis 500 and the eleven sanctioned Grand Prix internationals (South African, Monaco, Dutch, Spanish, French, Austrian, British, Italian, German, Canadian and United States), fit primarily into Groups 6 through 9. Most, however, come from the Group 8 Formula Racing Cars.

These are the cars that bring out our oohs and ahs of admiration and mean little more to the average car buff. Driven by the Jackie Stewarts, Mario Andrettis, Ronnie Petersons and Graham Hills, they have little effect on us except for the excitement they generate and the products, tested in their machines, that ultimately get into our Camaros, Firebirds, Mustangs and Road Runners.

Not so with the cars in the first five groups. These come closer to home, and represent what most car lovers consider the true function of automobile racing, developing four-wheelers we can all relate to and identify with, the cars being built that we can buy and drive. This is certainly true regarding the machines in Group 1, the stock cars we all know.

The ten-event Trans-Am Championship series run in 1971 points up the sizzling-hot competition between the muscle machines we see on American and Canadian roads every day. The ten events leading to the championship were held on race courses from Lime Park, Connecticut, to Riverside, California, with stops along the way at Laconia, New Hampshire; Lexington, Ohio; Edmonton, Alberta; Brainerd, Minnesota; Elkhart Lake, Wisconsin; Mont Tremblant, Quebec; Watkins Glen, New York; and Michigan's International Speedway in the Irish Hills.

Mustangs, Javelins, Camaros, Firebirds, Challengers, Tempests and Barracudas battled each other through a six-month period beginning in early May. The interesting point is that Javelin, the least popular in terms of cars sold, all but ran away with the competition. This pride of American Motors finished first in eight of the ten events, including a one-two and a one-two-three crossing of the finish line. Mustang racked up the other two wins.

Before you make any judgment as to the relative merits of the two cars consider this: Out of 81 Mustangs entered in the 10 Trans-Am races, 31 failed to finish in their races; of 28 Javelins entered in the competitions, ten failed to complete the events in which they were entered. In the over-all ten-race run, other than their wins, Mustang racked up a total of seven seconds, five thirds, five fourth places and two fifth finishes. Javelin's record was two third-place finishes, three each for third and fourth. No other make finished closer than third (Camaro twice) in all ten races.

Whatever you may make out of the isolated facts, it is significant that in seven of the eight races won by Javelin the driver was Mark Donohue. The eighth Javelin win was piloted by George Follmer, and it was Follmer who had been behind the wheel of the two Mustangs that handed Javelin its only defeats in the ten races. Follmer had switched to Javelin only for the final Trans-Am competition at Riverside on October 3, when Donohue was not available. In one of the two Mustang wins, Donohue and Javelin had finished second to Follmer.

In stock car racing, as suggested earlier, it's the driver's ability and the luck of the run, not the car alone, that gets the job done.

You may have an itch to race your muscle machine. You have great confidence in your car and in yourself. Is there a chance, then, for competition on an amateur basis? After all, the top thrill in muscle car ownership is racing. Only on the racetrack can you satisfy that nagging desire to settle for good whether or not you can make the right moves.

If you've got what it takes, the opportunity is there. The preliminaries are simple, but important. Your car must pass specific safety checks. You must have certain safety equipment and clothing that protects in the event of collision or fire.

Burnout on a Dragstrip

Image International, LA

As an amateur, whether you want to race for pleasure or for the cash that might be in it, there's but one place to start, the Sports Car Club of America. It is the only setup that permits, organizes and supervises amateur drivers on American ovals. Just as it does for the professionals, the SCCA sets up classes for amateur competition. There's no way they'll let you race your Jaguar against a Toyota. Everyone's got to have an even chance.

9

THE INDIVIDUAL DRAGSTER

You've got a sweet-running muscle machine and you'd like to have some fun with it, show off its zip and power. You don't see yourself as a pro prospect for the racing scene, but the urge is there all the same. The desire for action is eating at your insides. The question is: Where do you put the muscle pulsing under the bonnet of your pride and joy to work? What can you do, especially if you live in a dense metropolitan area?

You could join the car freaks who congregate after midnight on isolated neighborhood streets or just-out-of-town highway stretches that become temporary drag strips, but street racing in big cities has mushroomed to a point where the citizens are up in arms and the law is tougher and tougher.

It's a big problem, big in direct proportion to the city in which you live. For a few years now the residents of the suburbs just north of Detroit have made it hot for the hot-rodding dragster. Night after night, on the principal street leading north from the Detroit limits, Woodward Avenue, the dragsters had taken over. Through Royal Oak, Pleasant Ridge and plush Birmingham and Bloomfield Hills, the roar of revved up engines and the smell of burning rubber was a way of night life. Police action would only temporarily halt the noise and stench.

Similar difficulties exist in other large cities, with New York's dilemma most aggravating of all, a situation vividly pinpointed by Christopher Howard's article in the September, 1972, issue of *Car and Craft* magazine. Mr. Howard, on *The New York Times'* staff, originally wrote the piece for the *Times* but it was never published by the paper.

As explained by Mr. Howard in his article on the problem of street racing in New York City, the car buff there is handcuffed, particularly if he wants to see or take part in any

Las Vegas News Bureau

Off-the-road racing action.

type of automobile race. He faces no less than a 65-mile drive in slow-moving traffic to reach the nearest track, the drag strip at Center Moriches, a situation "which is a shame since the rest of the country seems to enjoy" racing so much. As Howard points out, he is referring to legal racing, and "there's another kind."

In the boroughs of Queens, Brooklyn and the Bronx, according to Howard, a "respectable racing underground" operates. The favorite drag strip is an overpass behind the World's Fair Marina, a locale that affords a beautiful, panoramic view of Long Island Sound, "with the runway lights of LaGuardia Airport reflected in the oil black of the water on one side, while the empty grayness of Shea Stadium looms like a monstrous ghost of the Circus Maximus" on the other.

"As a drag strip," Howard wrote, "it's rather less impressive. The overpass is four lanes wide, and because it connects four major arteries, it's nearly impossible to get away with blocking off more than the two westbound lanes. The driver getting ready to make a run there has got to be scared: he's got the competition almost rubbing sides with him on the narrow strip, a solid wall of spectators' cars on one side, a 25-foot drop on the other and a sharp uphill curve waiting at the end of the quarter. It's not ideal for drag racing.

"If you want to race in New York, though, this is where and how you do it. The money on a single run sometimes is as much as $8,000, not counting side bets, and this is where you have to go to win it."

New York City police, pointing out that a few nearby communities have eased the drag-racing problem by setting up legal tracks for drag racing, feel the Big City should do the same. Don't hold your breath waiting for such action in your town.

Outside New York, however, you're quite likely to find a come-join-in-the-fun drag strip within easy driving distance. Most of these strips put out the welcome mat and give first-time drag racers the red-carpet treatment. They'll help you learn the ropes and give you every assistance in getting started. There's really not too much you need to know.

Drag strips, wherever located, are built for the same purpose. Yet each has its own personality. The physical layouts often differ. You need only familiarize yourself with the spread and any rules the specific track may have. Otherwise, requirements are usually the same. The routines for entering the track and for competition racing have few variations.

If you're going out as a spectator, you naturally head for the parking field. If your hope is to take a turn at dragging, you aim for the pits after paying your admission fee and buying your pit entrance pass. Once that is taken care of, you get into an inspection lane for a once-over of your machine.

The inspection covers every possible item that bears on your personal and car safety. You must have seat belts and must use them. Your muscle machine gets a thorough going over, special care being given to the condition of wheels and tires, whether the lug nuts on wheels are tight and the amount of play in your brake pedal.

Having passed inspection, you fill out the classification card you received when you purchased your pit pass. Based on the information you put down, the inspector tags your machine with a number and indicates a competition classification that suits your experience or lack of it. Your next stop is the weigh-in station, and once you've cleared that requirement you make for the staging lane.

If you've never dragged before, now's the time for your

first biggie, making a practice run, a time trial to determine the e.t. (elapsed time) class in which you will compete. It's taken for granted that you know what it's all about. If not, you'd wisely have sat in the stands and carefully eyed other drivers to familiarize yourself with the routine.

So let's say you're on the starting grid with no car in front of you. It's all systems go. Now you go through your "burnouts," making a number of fast starts in low gear to heat your tires so that they provide maximum traction on your take-off.

Your burnouts completed, you're ready. The "Christmas tree," a string of lights actuated by across-the-lane beams to monitor the various stages of your drag competition, stares you in the face. As you enter the prestart beam your eye is fixed on the top of the "tree." Set in the beams and waiting for the "go" signal, a series of amber lights flash vertically, blinking on and off.

You inch forward in your lane, ready for the last light on the "tree" to send you surging. This is the "go," the green light, and you've timed yourself to be on the big move when it flashes. Now you're "smoking" down that quarter-mile strip, anxious to register the fastest possible time for the distance.

At the end of the quarter-mile chute you'll see three lights set in the middle of the track, the elapsed-time registry lights and the light that indicates your miles-per-hour speed during the distance. Your aim is to pass through the beams that actuate these lights and, by all means, avoid running into them.

Once you've passed through the beams, you remove your foot from the accelerator and slow down. You *don't* stomp on your brakes. When you have decelerated to a safe speed, you take the first turnout from the lane, and swing onto the road that parallels the drag strip and leads you back to the pits. Before you re-enter the pit area, you stop at a booth where you get the timed results of your drag. Your elapsed time, as well as your mph, is noted for you on a slip. These determine the classification in which you may compete. As a newcomer to the ranks you are, in this way, saved from being totally humiliated by a car and/or driver far superior to your machine and you.

Basic competition on the drag strip will be between you and a second car. Win your heat and, depending on your time results, you may find yourself in a higher classification. The object, as in any competition, is to be among the best of the best.

The world of drag racing is a wild, mad world. For you, as a once-in-a-while competitor or spectator, it can be loaded with fun. For the pro who travels the strips from New York to California, the fun and profit make worth-while the dangers and agonies of eating up 1,300 feet of blistering-hot asphalt straightaway in limited seconds. The power plant under his car's bonnet has to be strong enough to cope with repeated hard runs without overheating or stalling. The clutch, rear end and transmission have to prove themselves able to withstand tough use and abuse. It takes a lot of knowing and a lot of doing to put the blitz on that quarter-mile run.

Drag racers compete in a variety of categories. There are the stocks, which are divided into different classifications scaling down from the "pro stock" cars, those models off the assembly line usually raced under car maker sponsorship, to the stock model you might drive to work and drag on weekends.

Other categories include the "gas altered," considered to be the toughest, most nerve-wracking class in drag racing.

An "Altered" Dragster

Altered Dragster

They are officially named the Fuel Altereds, and the designation explains the specific difference, one that brings elapsed times in the low seven-second bracket and speeds of 200 miles per hour and more.

Another drag strip category is that of the "wheelstanders," a group especially popular with the multitudes who make up the spectator galleries. Usually competing during "down time" at major drag competitions, periods when for one reason or another actual drag races are not being run, these strange machines keep the crowd in its collective seat. Wheelstanders provide an unbelievably strange and amazing sight, surging down the quarter-mile lane of the drag strip on their rear wheels, with their front wheels lifted high like a rearing horse. A match race between two wheelstanders is something to see, two cars hurtling forward side by side at speeds approaching 150 miles per hour, their front ends reaching for the sky. Engines in the wheelstanders are mounted at the rear, usually in the trunk of the car.

Then there are the Funny Cars. The name is a mystery of sorts. The average fan is likely to say that they're "different," bringing on a laugh. Drag racing a Funny Car is no laughing matter, however. Their power plants are ordinarily at least 1,500-horsepower fuel-burning engines and, occasionally, you'll see a Funny Car on the drags sporting two high-powered engines.

The bodies of Funny Cars are plastic or Fiberglas. The cars are not stock models such as you might buy at a dealership, though they begin that way. The drag champions who race Funny Cars alter them as they please. A Ford chassis may have a Chevy, Plymouth Hemi or other engine under the bonnet. The transmission may be from a foreign car. Engine internals can be from a wide variety of manufacturers.

109

Image International, LA

VW "Altered" Wheelstander

Image International, LA

"Motown Missile"—Wheelstander

The Individual Dragster

Despite their name, Funny Cars mean big money to the promoters of the drags, keeping filled stands in a wild frenzy. These were the cars that brought high showmanship to the drags. The men who pilot them, all showmen at heart, have helped push the Funny Car category into a top attraction as a spectator sport. The cars they drive are hot in looks, painted in a rainbow of colors. Provocative names and saucy slogans invariably decorate the sides of the machine. Most are sponsored by commercial companies, many of which have nothing to do with the automobile industry.

A typical example of Funny Cars is the Texas Terror, driven by Bobby Streakley of Dallas, a member of the famous Coca Cola Cavalcade of Stars. Streakley's Camaro, body-painted in a gleaming deep purple highlighted by shades of red and purple, catches the eye the second it tools onto the track. Decals attesting to the sponsor as well as to suppliers of parts

Image International, LA

Funny Car Dragster

and components almost cover the front and rear fenders. The car is further streaked with white striping that starts in tapered lines at the trunk and hood areas and widens to a diamondlike spread that all but covers the door. Within this widened section, in fancy curlicued letters, is the name Bobby Streakley.

Streakley is a great favorite of drag fans because of his daring capers, including an exciting fire burnout that is banned at many tracks. Burnouts help in the heating of tires to increase traction on take-off. Fire burnouts, the belching from exhaust of sheets of flames that leap 15 to 20 feet to the rear of the car, is a starting-line antic that thrills the fans. Too often it also results in extensive damage to the vehicle. It is no longer permitted in races sanctioned by the National Hot Rod Association.

Funny Car fans are usually an excitable and loyal group. Each has a favorite, win or lose. The charm may be in the showmanship of the driver or his winning ways. Or it may be in the odd-ball name identifying his machine, carefully chosen to reflect the personality of the driver or that of the car.

Bruce Larson, a Pennsylvanian and one of the first to thrill fans with a mind-boggling fire burnout, may change cars, but his drag machines always carry broad red, white and blue stripes. Appropriately, the Larson Funny Car is named USA-1. Malcom Durham, of Hyattsville, Maryland, dubs his popular Funny the Strip Blazer.

Names of Funny Cars cover the waterfront in type and significance. Consider the following as just a drop on the drag strip of the thousands that stagger the imagination. The Sensuous, Cha Cha, Rat Trap, Chi Town Hustler, Motown Shaker, Bits & Pieces, The Snake, Grumpy's Toy, Quarter

Winged Express—Funny Car

"Grumpy's Toy"—Funny Car

Horse, Golddigger, Flying Red Baron and RRRRRevellution!

Some names are generated to have a specific meaning. The Mob, as one example, is an acronym formed of the first letters of the last name of two of its owners and the first name of the third: Ed Moore and Mike Bradley represent the M and B, while Omar Swoger supplies the O. Then there's Gary Kleckner's wheelstander, Chevado. With an Olds Toronado engine mounted in the rear of a Chevy Station Wagon, the "Chev" and last three letters of Toronado were combined— obvious, yet ingenious, and a colorful name for a Funny Car.

The drags are great fun even if you're only a spectator. If you've a mind to try it for yourself, you'll like it. Know your stuff first, however, and know your car and its (and your) limitations. There's plenty of help available if you look for it.

The ideal starting point is to join a hot-rod club. In almost every state of the union there are street rod associations made up of car buffs just like you. Many are affiliated with the National Street Rod Association (NSRA), with headquarters in Studio City, California. These are your best bets. Membership in NSRA as well as in a local club not only helps you but also gives strength to an organization created to further the sport.

The NSRA is not a commercial, fast-buck setup. It wages a continual fight against such groups on both local and national levels and will help keep you clear of organizations that offer nothing in return for a high dollar. The NSRA membership fee is surprisingly low—just $5 annually in the United States and $6 outside—and, in this writer's opinion, gives you back two to three times the amount in immediate benefits: an identification card honored at all respectable drag strips; two decals for your car; a full year's subscription to a fine publication called *Street Scene*, which keeps you up to date on local as well as national drag competitions and what may be the going-thing in components, equipment and restrictions; and "anything you need help on" service to individual members as well as to local clubs.

Magazines devoted to the drag scene also give the newcomer to the strips invaluable help. Providing expert how-what-where information, this wide range of publications will be considered in a later chapter.

Looking at the broad picture, it seems as though everybody's taking an increasing interest in drag racing. The University of Akron recently added a noncredit summer course that covered "speed performance" in addition to custom painting, machine repair and engine construction. Dubbed "Drag Racing 101," the course at the Ohio university is being seriously considered as a permanent credit-earning study. It may well be that other universities will follow suit.

Drag strip owners, too, are beginning to take a long, hard look at the value of strengthening interest of young people in the sport. Two West Coast drag strips, the Irwindale Raceway and the Orange County International, just southwest of Los Angeles, have initiated High School Scholarship Drags.

These competitions are limited to high-school students. Participants compete as teams representing their schools. Interest by individuals and schools has been tremendous. Hotrod associations and lawmen alike are hoping that strips in all areas of the country will follow suit as one way to discourage illegal on-street dragging by car freaks who have nowhere else to show off their muscle machines.

10

FUN IS WHERE YOU FIND IT

Owning a sweet-running muscle machine, you're naturally in love with it right down to its tire tread. Just as naturally you like to show it off, to demonstrate what it can do and how adept you are as a driver. The drag strip is only one of many ways to go for the muscle car buff.

Taking part in a gymkhana is another exacting, exciting way in which you can swing with the car loving crowd. In the gymkhana muscle as such takes a back seat. Your driving skill and the ease of handling of your car rate number one. It's a test of your ability to throttle, shift and brake your way through a complex maze of lanes formed by a series of pylons. It's like going on four wheels through a man-made obstacle course that boggles your mind. But it's great fun.

Gymkhanas may be held in almost any wide paved area. Shopping center parking lots are among the most used—even today, when many such centers are open on Sundays. Gymkhana courses demand open areas, and some shopping complexes will close off one section of their parking lots in order to generate traffic from gymkhana spectators. Rarely is there a charge for watching a gymkhana.

The parking area chosen for the course is marked off in lanes separated by pylons and lines. The drivers who compete are required to negotiate the laid-out maze of lanes through the lines and around pylons in a race with time. A typical course includes slalom-type straightaways around pylons, high-speed 180-degree turns, open and sharp turns, figure eights and chicanes, which, evolving from the word "chicanery," call for maneuverability through unexpectedly tricky setups.

Entries totaling two hundred or more for a single meet are not unusual. All, of course, do not compete at the same time. Yet so many may be included in a single run that the effect, for the spectator, is that of watching a swarm of giant-size bugs dashing in all directions at the same time. For the man in the machine it's a matter of speeding, turning, braking and shifting gears again and again through a course made intentionally challenging, but not impossible.

It may look easy to weave your way through twenty or more pylons at speeds approaching a hundred miles per hour. It is anything but. It takes perfect timing, which comes only from exhaustive practice, to gracefully execute this slalom on land without crashing through the pylons. Smooth coordination between acceleration, braking and maneuvering is what it takes to complete a gymkhana course with an undented car.

Unlike the drag strip or racing oval, the gymkhana has no lengthy straightaways and no banked curves. Nor do you have an opportunity to make practice runs to familiarize yourself with the course, analyze its tricky turns and bends and plan your course of action. You come to the competition

117

Car given the flag to enter gymkhana competition.

Gymkhana competitor making it through the pylons.

cold, with only your driving ability and natural reflexes to guide you during your first run, a chase against the ticks of time.

Most gymkhana championships, however, are decided on the average scores racked up during three turns over the course. Many drivers will take their first run all out to determine the speed with which they can make most turns in the course and which areas may cause trouble. Second runs may be somewhat slower as they correct mistakes made on the first run-through. In the third and final run it's again all out and utilizing the experience and information gained during the first two turns.

The true gymkhana enthusiast runs the course like the expert on the ski slopes, his action smooth and steady, however slow or fast he pushes his machine. He doesn't swing

Albert J. Bizer

An unusual gymkhana—slalom on a snow course.

into the course with throttle wide open so that sudden braking is called for.

The best time made in the three runs is the key to winning. Equally important as time are the abilities to make it through two pylon "gates" without touching or knocking the pylons over and making quick turns without braking or sliding. Failures mean additions to your best time, five seconds added to final time for each failure to make it between two pylons and two seconds for each pylon barely touched.

Wherever you live, you're bound to find a sports car club that conducts gymkhana competitions throughout the year except in the "snow" months. Some clubs require membership to participate in their gymkhanas, but most welcome outsiders. Responsible organizations conducting a gymkhana insist that cars entered in their competition pass technical inspections covering suspension, brakes and steering.

Rallyes, which may take any of many forms, are another form of fun competition for the car buff who's not about to make racing his profession. They are held the year 'round in Southern areas and through six to nine months in the North. Almost anyone, in any type of car, can take part in a rallye —and the more, the merrier.

The rallye is not a race *against* time but, rather, a challenge to keep pace with the ticking hands of a clock, to finish as close to a preset finishing time as possible. Usually it takes two to rallye, the driver and a navigator. It is an ideal sport for "couple" enjoyment.

Weekends are the usual rallye times. Preset routes are mapped, usually on public roads. Often predetermined speeds are also set and must be averaged by the competitors at the conclusion of the run. In a rallye the navigator is at least as important as the driver. He (or she) interprets

CONTROL - ST. IGNACE OUT - 14 Min/7.17 Miles

.00	LEFT ONTO STATE STREET
.12	R X R
1.2	BEAR RIGHT FOR MACKINAC BRIDGE
2.33	FARE BOOTH - PAY TOLL OF $1.50
6.7	EXIT RIGHT FROM I 75 AT FIRST OPPORTUNITY AFTER CROSSING THE BRIDGE
6.89	LEFT TOWARD "WILDERNESS PARK"
7.03	LEFT AT STOP ONTO CENTRAL STREET
7.14	STRAIGHT AT TRAFFIC LIGHT ACROSS NICOLET STREET
7.15	RIGHT INTO TOTAL STATION
7.17	CONTROL - MACKINAW CITY IN - TOTAL GASOLINE AVAILABLE - TAKE 15 MINUTES TO REFUEL
7.17	CONTROL - MACKINAW CITY OUT - 35 Min/43.08 Miles
7.18	LEFT OUT OF TOTAL STATION ONTO CENTRAL STREET
7.22	STRAIGHT AT TRAFFIC LIGHT ACROSS NICOLET STREET (WEST)
7.33	RIGHT TOWARD I 75
7.48	RIGHT AT YIELD
7.54	KEEP RIGHT AND ENTER I 75 SOUTH
17.35	"REST AREA 1 MILE"
36.4	EXIT RIGHT FROM I 75 AT THE M 68 EXIT FOR INDIAN RIVER
36.69	RIGHT AT STOP
36.73	RIGHT ONTO CLUB ROAD *****
37.30	RIGHT AT YIELD ONTO ONAWAY ROAD
38.90	LEFT ONTO COXEY ROAD AND FOLLOW PAVEMENT
42.07	RIGHT ONTO SILERY ROAD
42.83	KEEP LEFT AND GO UP THE HILL
43.08	T CONTROL - SCOTT'S BAY - 1 Min/43.19 Miles
43.19	START CONTROL - SILERY ROAD M STAGE - 3 Min/45.92 Miles
43.20	KEEP RIGHT

Sample page, rallye instructions

the instructions and route directions and keeps a check on time—all vital factors in naming the rallye winner, especially when the car must finish as near as possible to the designated average speed. Teamwork between driver and navigator keeps the rallye competitor on course and on time.

The Sports Car Club of America sanctions annual National Championship events in two separate rallye classes. One is a straight competition in which instrument use—compasses, computers, etc.—is not permitted. The second is planned for cars equipped with sophisticated instruments.

Fun and kicks is the name of the rallye game. Rallyes can take the form of any of many variations and gimmicks. Rallyes with such odd-ball names as poker run, hare and hounds and beach bummer are popular. In the run you may find coded signs along the route. If you can't decipher the code, you're in trouble. Some rallyes include a scavenger hunt to add interest.

Scoring for most rallyes is on a demerit system, where a specified number of points are deducted for various goofs or for every minute you miss the finish "perfect time." The fewer the mistakes and the closest you are to the preset finish time, the surer you are of winning.

The rallye is the one event that brings the greatest number of club members together. It does far more. Participants can be anybody and everybody, which provides the excuse for devoting more space to the detailed hows and whats of rallyeing typified by the biggest and most popular, Michigan's POR.

POR stands for Press On Regardless, which aptly describes the kind of event this international rallye truly is. The hundreds of contestants push on toward the finish despite any problems that might arise. If an engine conks out there's a hustle to diagnose the trouble and fix it. If a car gets mired in mud, sand or snow, push, strain, rock until it's free and you're again on your way.

As the SCCA describes it, a rallye is "a trip over the meadow and through the woods to grandmother's house when you don't know where she lives or how to get there, but you must be on time." In the POR rallye, grandma's house is a long way off—1500 miles in 1971, expanded to 2,000 miles for the 1972 event.

Nineteen seventy-two marks the 24th running of the POR test of car endurance and human skill in a long race against time to be run within legal speed limits. There's no way of dictating actually how fast is too fast. There's a lot of ground to cover, hundreds of obstacles to overcome, but you had better not be much ahead of schedule at the finish. That would be a sure tip that you didn't honor the posted speed limits. There's seldom any danger of any car finishing too fast, what with all the obstacles and problems. You'd more likely be concerned about the penalty points for finishing too far behind the estimated time for finish.

An important rallye such as the POR has a very detailed instructional time schedule, with a copy for each competing car. It is this schedule, divided into three sections—one for each of the three stages of the POR—which your companion, the navigator, watches closely in order to relay directions as you drive.

All three stages of the POR, except for the start of stage one, are run at night. Other daytime hours are used for rest layovers. It would seem that night driving would be impractical on the rough, twisting roads which make up a POR course.

"Safety is the reason for nights," Naomi Moothart, Activities Director for the SCCA Detroit Region, pointed out. "Headlights warn drivers of other cars in the woods. Besides, there's almost no non-rallye traffic in the woods at that time and, if a rallye car is in trouble the on-and-off flash of headlights tells course workers that somebody needs help. In winter the gleam of a car's lights in the woods can be seen for miles."

Rated by rallye enthusiasts to surpass even the Monte Carlo and East African rallyes, the POR is dubbed the meanest, longest, richest event of its kind in the world. Prizes range to $10,000.

Eighty-eight entries, including twenty different makes of cars from twenty-three states, three Canadian Provinces and one team from Italy made up the 1972 POR field.

The starting point on November 2, 1972, at ten in the morning, was on Belle Isle, an island park in the Detroit River near downtown Detroit.

The first course was a full twenty-four hour run with a four-mile scheduled initial run through the winding trails and woods of the island cut to one hour because of a steady rain-fall. The island tour was shortened so as not to damage the horse-riding paths. The teams moved out from the island starting line at one-minute intervals, made the mile island turn and crossed the bridge into Detroit, but not before a near misfortune.

Randy Black and his navigator, Tom Burgess, had come all the way from British Columbia for the rallye. They had driven their Datsun 3,000 miles to Detroit with no trouble, but the moment they pulled away from the starting line in the Belle Isle woods the bolts supporting the car's rear suspension fell apart. Black kept going for the mile island run, crossed the bridge and stopped.

There's no holding up a confirmed rallye bug. He and

Burgess, with the help of other rallye enthusiasts, went quickly to work and were soon back in the running, heading north on freeways, surface highways and side roads, hoping to overtake the luckier starters. They made it into 13th spot by the time the field paused for its first rest period, some three-quarters the distance of the first day's run.

That first lap was one of 750 miles, a preset winding, twisting course through Michigan's lower peninsula to St. Ignace, just across the bridge in the upper peninsula, ordinarily only a 310 mile trip. At the conclusion of the first day's run the leader was a former European rallye champion, Harry Kelstrom of Sweden, and his navigator/co-driver Britisher John Davenport, driving an Italian Lancia.

The Kelstrom-Davenport team enjoyed an eight minute lead over the second placers, Michigan's Jim Walker and Terry Palmer in a Volvo. A Datsun piloted by Tom Jones and Ralph Beckman was third, with Gene Henderson and Ken Pogue, in an AMC Waggoneer, fourth.

Following a twelve hour layover in St. Ignace, the second stage of the POR got under way after dark. This led the entries into what is referred to as an "M" Stage—"M for Murderous" as the drivers dub it. It was all of that, swinging through pitted and potted logging trails of Northern Michigan's Hiawatha National Forest. Added to the natural hazards of bad roads, drizzle and freezing rain, there was also an almost blind search for a tank-truck fuel stop at five in the morning—as noted on the printed schedule—"somewhere near Germfask." One's guess was as good as the next's. This second stage, a circular swing that started north to Lake Superior and then curved back south almost to the Lake Michigan shore, ended back at St. Ignace.

After another rest layover the third night's action led back across the Mackinaw Bridge into lower Michigan and through more of the northern wilds of the Lower Peninsula. The finish line was reached about noon Sunday after a south-ward route that snaked about 700 miles to Alma in central lower Michigan. Only twenty-one of the original starters crossed the finish line.

The surprise winners were Henderson and Pogue—one a police sergeant, the other an airport flight instructor—in their AMC Jeep Waggoneer. In second place, crossing the finish line eight minutes later, were Jones and Beckman in their Datsun 240Z. Another four minutes behind came two other Michiganders, Erhard Lahm and Jim Callon in a second AMC Jeep Waggoneer.

Henderson and Pogue were as surprised as anyone at their win.

"There are two parts to a road rallye like this," Henderson said. "The rough part and the frightening part. The rough part is the sand, mud, water, rocks and trees that block your path—part of every rallye. The frightening part is the need to make these hazards at car-breaking speeds. We made it through the frightening parts, because the Jeep took the hazards faster than the fragile, even if faster, sports cars."

The ideal rallying car weighs about 2,000 pounds and pushes between 150 and 200 horsepower. It can accelerate to 100 miles an hour in 20 seconds.

"That's why we didn't think we had a chance to make it," Henderson said. "Our Jeep weighs 4800 pounds and has about 260 horsepower. It would take a half day or so to get up to that 100 miles an hour."

An interesting note is that among the 21 cars which finished the POR all but three makes—AMC Jeep twice, Dodge Colt and AMC Gremlin once each—were foreign imports. These included the Japanese Datsun, with ten finishing among the 21, the Japanese Subaru with two, Germany's

Volvo with two, Japan's Toyota and Mazda with one each and Sweden's SAAB with one.

Though Michigan's lumber trails and backroads washed out so many—some with steering difficulties, others with braking, suspension and engine difficulties—most will be back for another go at this toughest of all road rallyes. Next time there may be no slowing down to avoid hitting a porcupine, deer or bear; no getting permanently mired in mud and snow. With all the hazards there's a thrill in rallying that keeps one hoping for another chance.

One important fact should not be overlooked, however. To enjoy a rallye in safety—especially one as rugged and demanding as the POR—the event must be well organized and well supervised. And organization and supervision is best done by an experienced sports car club.

It takes know-how and love of the game to develop instructions, set-up checkpoints and prescribed times—no more, no less—in which to complete a course. Hard work is necessary to write and print route sheets and timing cards, to initiate and enforce safety rules and provide the officials needed.

Sports car clubs have the know-how and the man-power. Club members love their cars, love what they can do with them. They pass on to newcomers all the little details that develop driving and navigational skills. One cannot join a sports car club without being thoroughly involved.

There are other ways to actively enjoy that zoomie you take pride in. There is the one-against-the-clock type of event, in which an individual contestant goes through a maneuverability test over a set course. The fastest time with no incident assures a win—it's usually that tough. Hill climbs and time trials are similar types of competition.

For those who want participation without active competi-

Lineup of cars awaiting the start of POR Rallye

Stopping at a rallye checkpoint for further instructions.

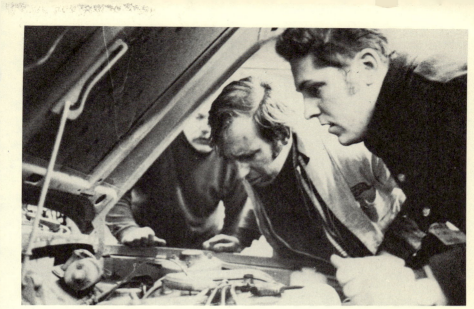

Engine trouble during POR Rallye

Through a backwoods logging trail during POR Rallye

Competitors assist a team mired in deep sand during POR Rallye.

1971 POR Rallye winners crossing the finish line at Alma, Michigan.

Competitor approaching a hill climb grade.

tion, there are the many car shows, a comparatively new type of event that has increased in popularity with both spectators and participants. This is not the big splash and heavily advertised car exhibit held in huge arenas, the manufacturer-sponsored affair ballyhooed at new-model time each fall. It is a show for you and me, called "Concour," where cars are judged in compatible groups for their closeness to new condition.

Concours are usually held in a rural area, where the green of the grass and trees and the blue of the sky make a fitting background for gleaming, polished-spotless automobiles. Group competitions are set up separately for antique sports cars, classic cars, older cars still being driven daily, cars of specific mileage or age or condition and competition muscle models.

There is a definite bending over backwards to be fair in these show competitions. Cars that are used daily get special allowances for natural driving hazards, such as stone dents. Basic cleanliness is the big thing, calling for a heavy expenditure of elbow grease in cleaning and waxing. When you love your machine, it's anything but work.

If you're like most car enthusiasts, you want action of one kind or another to thoroughly enjoy your sports machine. It's not enough for you to zip through a superhighway with one eye on the speedometer and the other on the rear-view mirror, or to climb a challenging peak with nobody to admire the smoothness that marks the climb of your muscle machine.

Whichever way you go, however you want to show off that shiny pride in the driveway, the choice is yours. If it's action you want, there's at least one that will suit your special urge.

11

FUNTASTIC WAYS TO GO:
SWAP/RESTORE

Though they have little to do directly with the muscle machines turned out by the men in Detroit, the swap and restore hang-ups are another big expression of man's love for his wheels. Neither are really new, but both have enjoyed a high swing back into popularity, especially with the younger crowd.

Swapping—the substitution of a more powerful engine— was a big thing with rodders and other car bugs some twenty years ago. Beginning in the 1950s, when the car buyer could order a high-performance engine as an option for his new car and have it installed by the manufacturer, swapping took a back seat.

One of the reasons for the recent big swing back to swapping is the air pollution squelch placed on the production of high-performance engines. Another, and older, reason is the mushrooming insurance rate, which makes protecting anything but a family car almost impossible unless you have a corner on the mint.

133

MAG WHEELS AND RACING STRIPES

Add the fact that rodders traditionally prefer wheels that are as unlike what can be bought in a dealership as thinking can make them, and you have another swap motive. Still another is the mother lode of great muscle-ready engines that can be found in the car junkyards of America.

For whatever reason the individual car freak does it, there's a big do these days in taking a lightweight car like Pinto, Vega, Dart and Gremlin and giving it a shot of hard muscle by switching its engine to a three- or four-year-old power plant that may have rested under the bonnet of a discarded 'Vet, Bird or other high-performance machine. It also costs a lot less, is more practical and results, in the long run, in a better set of wheels than if one were to try hopping up the smaller engine.

Engine swapping is not limited to the newer, small cars. As much, perhaps more, is made in old, classic model cars, including the now historic and almost legendary Ford T, most of which more appropriately fit in the "restoring" scene.

Should you get bit by the swapping bug, there are guidelines to keep you on the straight road to making a sensible and practical conversion. One thing is certain. You don't start out by installing just any engine into any car you might have handy. Swaps that don't do a job aren't worth the first second's work you put into them.

Say you've got a 1939 Ford or 1969 Datsun chassis. You're not about to put in a 429-cubic-incher. Equally out of line would be swapping the 427 from a 1967 Corvette for a Boss 302. Granted these are exaggerated examples, but they make the point clear. You start out by selecting an engine that is physically compatible with the engine compartment space, and with the car itself.

A tight fit won't do, either. There must be sufficient clearance for easy access to spark plugs and enough room to accommodate headers and exhaust manifold and provide for breathing space around the gear box and steering column. To save future headaches that may never go away, it is advisable to live with the original steering system designed for the car.

The weight of the replacement engine is another important consideration. The new engine may be heavier than the original one, but not by too many pounds. Compensation for small increases in weight can be achieved by installing stiffer front springs. An engine that is too heavy may seriously affect the maneuverability of the vehicle.

Before making a final decision as to the engine, you must consider the use you expect to get from the vehicle in which the engine is to be installed. If normal day-to-day driving is what you want, you are more likely to be happy with a job under 350 cubic inches. For racing purposes, as long as the chassis can handle it, you can go for the power plant over 450 cubic inches.

There's more, of course, to making an effective swap than merely having the selected engine installed in the vehicle. Naturally you must be sure that the frame of the car is strong enough to support the mounts for the engine transplant. Using the mounts specified by the manufacturer of the engine is the safest course, even though it may mean extra work of getting brackets capable of handling the new mounts.

Other questions that must be answered before you have a smoothly operating vehicle are those relating to the transmission. Here again, compatibility with the engine is vital. Again, your choice of automatic or manual transmission should depend on the use you hope to make of the converted car. If you're not intending to race or drag, the automatic will be preferable, especially if the unit already includes automatic transmission and the new engine will bolt directly to it.

If the engine you are installing is appreciably larger or more powerful than the original, it may call for a larger radiator to guarantee sufficient cooling. Proper exhaust manifolds should be considered as well and—if high performance is your aim—the use of headers is necessary.

Kits, including the components you will need, are now available for most of the popular engines. They are usually prefabricated for inclusion in specific model cars; if the chassis you have is one for which these prefab kits are available, you have it made. If you don't want to go the kit route, there's always the nearest salvage yard. Somewhere close by, if you're lucky, you will find exactly what you need to finish your engine swap job.

Altered Pick-up on Dragstrip

Image International

The "restorer" is a somewhat different breed from the swapper. His great passion is finding an old model—the older, the better—and restoring it to as near its original, bought-from-a-dealer condition as his love of cars can make it. A restored Model T is very likely the big dream of 99 per cent of those who get involved with cars in this challenging way, a way that has boomed sky high in the past few years.

Restoring is a bit like turning a lemon into lemonade. You find what may be the rusting body and chassis of a '29 Model A, a '39 Chevy coupe or an early "T"—the earlier, the better—and get to work. Once you might have picked up your choice at a local junkyard, but restoring has become a big thing. Now, even if you are lucky enough to spot one at Sam's Salvage, you won't take it home for a song. Sam has likely wised up to the building interest in restoring and may want an arm and a leg for a grim something with mangled fenders and hood.

In far-back rural areas, discarded oldsters are still to be found and had almost for the taking, but it requires a lot of travel and looking. The smart restorer now heads for a restorers' or swappers' meet, which may be held sometime during the year not too far from home. There he'll find car buffs from miles around who bring what they don't need and are ready to sell or swap for another item they may have a use for.

The most famous and largest of these swappers' meets is the annual restorers and swappers get-together at Harrah's in Reno, Nevada. A big side attraction is Harrah's Museum, a prestigious display of shiny restoreds. You can drool over the like-new antiques behind the velvet ropes, but it's out on the meet grounds that you might bargain for the start of your own restored.

137

MAG WHEELS AND RACING STRIPES

What you find, either at Harrah's or at a gathering closer to home, will be only the start, perhaps a broken, beat and bent original chassis that, with your eyes closed, you visualize as rivaling the finest you saw inside the museum. Or it may be that you already have the chassis and now you find a body that might well have graced that frame you own. It may need work—bumping out dents, sanding, smoothing and applying twenty to thirty coats of paint—but there it is and you want it. You begin your dicker, and your dream is on the way to fulfillment.

At a restorers' meet, such as the annual Harrah's, you find complete and partially complete vintage models that can get you started on a restoring kick in nothing flat. Engines, hoods, fenders, components and instrument panels—almost anything an oldster once sported—is bound to be there. Prices can vary from the reasonable to the ridiculous. A "good condition" Model-T fuel tank at $6 and fair-to-good front fenders for a T at $25 make sense. Not so $150 for dented doors or $750 for a '40 Chevy coupe that wasn't all there. Yet, if you're a good bargainer and know your stuff, you can make it.

Restoring an old-timer to its original condition is hard, time-consuming work, but it's a weekend labor of love for the buff who digs cars. Once that T Roadster is all together, its vintage tin as shiny black as when it first rolled down a rutted road two lifetimes ago, it's all worthwhile. The look of envy from that Mach I you pass says everything.

In almost every state you'll find tours and runs to show off your new oldster, with prizes to help compensate for the hours and dollars you poured into your dream. You needn't go far from home to display that pride you put so much into, but if you've got the vacation time and can swing the distance there's the annual run and tour through Yellowstone National Park, held each summer since 1969.

They come from as far away as eastern Canada and as close as West Yellowstone, Wyoming, the village on the park outskirts where the run begins. A hundred and more traditional and vintage restoreds usually register for the tour, and perhaps half as many join in the fun without putting their names on the official roll.

Nineteen twenty-eight touring cars, '29 roadsters, '31 sedans, '39s, '40s and a raft of in-betweens parade leisurely between the towering trees of Yellowstone, past Old Faithful, the endless blue of Yellowstone Lake, thermal basins, delicate formations and sun-bathed pools. When the tour is completed, awards are made in a number of categories. These include the Open Fender Class, Most Popular Nonfender, Most Popular Sedan and Over-all Most Popular. A special

Detroit Public Library

1929 MG Midget

award is given the registered driver who has come the longest distance to the meet. It's all fun and pleasure, including the surprised stares of bear, moose and bison as the cars make their way through the winding roads.

Another heavily attended annual get-together is the combined roadster-restoreds' and swappers' Father's Day exhibit in the Los Angeles area. Begun in 1964, this happening plays to filled grandstands every year and attracts rodders and swappers from wherever. Many who make the Yellowstone get to the L.A. meet as well.

Aisles filled with restored oldsters are roped off to keep the lookers from touching. In other parts of the grounds, hundreds of "swap" items are displayed and waiting for takers, complete and partial vehicles, engines, transmissions, components, what-have-you. Too many, as at most swap meets, are rough in quality and far overpriced, but the sharp-eyed and shrewd buyer can often help himself to what he needs.

There's a load of excitement in restoring or swapping. With muscle fading from the scene so far as the Detroit makers are concerned, this is one area in the wheels scene that's on the interest upgrade.

12

THE WORLD OF MUSCLE:
A READER'S PARADISE

From his earliest years, the young American has a fascination for cars that nothing can erase. By the time the teens are reached, this itch for wheels is beyond control and not satisfied until the car in his dream future has become a reality. New or old, it matters little.

The urge to know what makes a car tick comes early and it, too, is seldom satisfied, for there is always something new to look into. Books on the automobile have always been big with the young crowd, and there are books covering almost every type of automobile ever manufactured—classic cars, vintage cars, sports cars, foreign cars.

When the racing scene blossomed out to include hot rodding, dragging and the many other competitions that made cars fun, books were not enough. Things changed too fast, and young America wanted to know *right now* just what was going on.

In 1947 hot rodding made its first impact on the sports

scene. The young had been converging from the southwestern areas of the United States on the sandy stretches of Southern California to try out their hopped-up wheels. Attending these early get-togethers was a young man named Robert Petersen. He heard the talk, the interminable questions being asked, and decided that what these young people hooked on automobiles needed was a regular magazine to answer their questions and keep them abreast of changes in the automobile industry.

Petersen, farsighted and a young man of action, wasn't about to let someone beat him to a potentially powerful idea. He wasted no time. The result was *Hot Rod,* the first magazine of its kind. Still growing in popularity after 25 years of publication, *Hot Rod* is the bible of the drag and race crowd. A typical issue carries features on the top competitions of the previous month, technical articles on how to build a street machine, dragster, funny car or whatever, what to do and what not to do. It will include special pieces on individual cars and drivers who have contributed to the racing picture.

Bob Petersen didn't stop with *Hot Rod.* He saw the need for other and varied approaches to the automobile's place in American life. Two years after the birth of *Hot Rod* he produced *Motor Trend,* another monthly that keeps a sharp eye on developments in the industry. In 1953 *Car Craft,* concentrating on the how-to-do-it, made its bow, followed by *'Teen, Rod & Custom, Hot Rod Industry News* and *Wheels Afield,* as well as a group devoted to aspects of transportation other than automobiles.

Obviously Bob Petersen knew what he was doing. The first issue of *Hot Rod,* for example, totaled 5,000 copies. Today a single issue can run as high as a million or more.

Petersen Publishing, with headquarters in Los Angeles and

offices throughout the country, has had tremendous impact on racing as well as on the automobile industry as a whole. Each of the Petersen publications is staffed by experts in a specific field who have campaigned year-in, year-out for better racing conditions and a better automotive product. Petersen, as the magazine *Business Week* described him in a personality piece, is the one who educated a whole generation of young drivers.

As would be expected, others have come along to add to the wealth of reading material about the muscle, drag and race scenes. Argus Publications, also out of Los Angeles, now publishes *Popular Hot Rodding, Custom & Rod* and *Off Road Vehicles* as regulars, with special one-timers occasionally to cover specific related subjects.

There are others, of course. Among the best are *Drag Racing USA, Car and Driver, Super Stock* and *Road & Track,* from a variety of publishers.

All of these magazines do much more than merely report on cars and racing. For the average car buff their greatest value perhaps comes from the advice columns which are a feature in almost all of these publications. Technical experts answer specific questions sent in by readers, questions that other readers will also find helpful.

John Dianna's monthly column in *Hot Rod* is an example of this type of "how-to" help. In a recent issue, a reader requested information on the right way to file piston ring ends when fitting them into the cylinder bores. Another reported that he was experiencing a heating problem he couldn't locate in his '67 Camaro with a 350 engine and asked whether a cooling recovery system would help.

Rod & Custom carries a similar service in its Bench Session, by John Thawley. One reader wrote Thawley saying he was considering installation of a small block Chevy engine in a '54 Studebaker coupe because he was looking for more power and reliability, and wondered if there wasn't a kit available to help him complete the installation. In the same column another reader asked if there was an easy way to remove a broken stud or bolt from a block.

Whatever the magazine and whatever the question, the answer is given clearly and helpfully. As you can see from the few examples mentioned, the breadth of advice offered is as broad as the inner workings of any automobile.

If, like most car buffs, you prefer taking care of your own machine and nursing it through its aches and pains personally, one of these magazines is bound to help you toward your M.D. in mechanics. If racing is your bag, as either participant or spectator, you'll get the low-down on the big races and the star racers, and you'll know where to go and what you need to do to make the big time on oval and drag strip.

The swapper and the restorer will find even more help in these publications. Space in many is made available to private individuals without cost for listing what they have to offer and/or what they need to make that old hunk of history found in the local salvage yard come alive.

With the many expected changes dictated by government control and by the auto makers' concern for their profit balance, it will be more important than ever to keep up with what's right and what's doing.

13

WHAT'S IN OUR FUTURE?

January 1, 1975, is D day for the automobile industry, the or-else day when the automobile makers must meet the government's tough exhaust emission standards. Too tough, say the car big-wigs. It can't be done.

How this tug-of-war will end, no one knows. What the future holds for the muscle/performance car is equally up in the air. No two automotive experts agree on the answer.

The one sure thing is that there is a sort of revolution now going on in the automobile business, one that entails a lot more than the traditional redesigning of a car for a new model year. Power and performance are important to the car-buying public, and the emission standards set by the government influence both tremendously. The car makers must produce a car the public will buy. It's important to them as businessmen, and important to the entire country because of its effect on the economy.

The major automobile manufacturers wish there was some

way to have the best of both worlds. They are all spending, and have already spent, millions of dollars trying to find a way out of the dilemma.

Many of them feel that the automobile industry has become a whipping-boy for headline-hunting politicians. To some degree, they may be right. At the beginning of the ecology hassle, around 1950, the internal combustion engine was blamed for contributing as much as 80 per cent to air pollution.

The auto makers declared that the figure was being blown far out of proportion. They made extensive tests on their own to prove their point, and the federal government, in the late '60s, finally set the figure at 39 per cent of man-made pollutants being directly attributable to the internal combustion engine that powers almost all automobiles.

Of course even 39 per cent is too much. Yet fairness dictates that one should consider the total picture. New cars being manufactured, even those made back when the flap got started, are not so much to blame for the high level of pollutants as older cars which have not been adequately cared for by their owners.

This was dramatically demonstrated in the spring of 1970 by mechanical engineering students at the University of Michigan. They conducted a one-day tune-up project on 43 automobiles built between 1962 and 1969 with speedometer mileages registering between 13,000 and 108,000 miles.

Before the cars were tuned, each was tested to see what their as-is pollution levels were. Then each car was given a thorough engine tune-up. Spark plugs were replaced, points were reset and carbon was cleaned out. After the engine tune-up the cars were retested for pollutant emissions and the result compared with the figure before tune-up.

The comparisons floored everybody concerned. After tune-up the cars showed a reduction of an average of 55 per cent in unburned hydrocarbons when engines were run at idle speeds, the point when emissions are highest. The tested cars also revealed a reduction in carbon monoxide levels of a whopping 90 per cent. In all, 85 per cent of the vehicles tested and tuned showed substantial reductions in the pollutant emissions that everybody had been crying about.

The evidence seems clear. The real pollution-spreading criminals in the automobile field were those not being given recommended care, whether they were being driven by people who just carelessly let them go or by those who just didn't have the money to keep their cars in tip-top shape. Yet all cars were being blamed equally, even the new.

Even before legislation came about, individual manufacturers began researching means to reduce even the minimal emissions for which new cars were being censured. Crankcase ventilation systems and other emission controls were installed in new cars, reducing even the minimal pollutants the best-tuned internal combustion engine would emit. Unburned hydrocarbons dropped 80 per cent from the earlier new-car emissions and carbon monoxide almost 70 per cent. Putting the comparison in a different way, *five* 1970 models emitted no more hydrocarbons than *one* 1960 model, and *three* 1970s discharged no more carbon monoxide than *one* new car of 1960.

The fight against the automobile, in Congress and in the press, went on just the same and still continues. The one thing certain is that with emission controls as they are legislated today for automobiles, there can no longer be the kind of performance or muscle machine that has taken the world by storm.

Stock engines now being built are designed to use only regular gasoline. The various emission controls being added to the engines cut down on power, and mean more complicated engines that demand more expert tuning more often. The result is a car that uses more fuel, gives less performance and costs far more initially to buy as well as to keep in shape during day-to-day driving.

The why of this reduced performance and increased cost revolves around two primary elements in the internal combustion engine. One is the air pump; the other is exhaust gas recirculation. The air pump, driven by the fan belt, injects fresh air into the exhaust manifold to help complete combustion. It acts like a parasite, eating up potential power and cutting about six horsepower from the engine's capability. Exhaust gas recirculation refers to the injection of exhaust gas, a conveniently inert gas, into the intake manifold. Since it won't burn, this gas lowers the temperature at which combustion occurs in the cylinders and reduces the oxides of nitrogen, which must be controlled in order to hold down harmful pollutant emission.

Since the internal combustion engine is called the real culprit in pollutant emissions, there has been a lot of talk about making a switch to other types of engines. The Wankel engine, powered by rotors as against piston power of the internal combustion, made the headlines as the possible savior of the automobile industry. Ford and General Motors have both made exhaustive tests on the possibilities offered by the Wankel, but it remains a question mark. The fact is that as far back as the early '60s the Wankel was already touted as the future engine to make all others obsolete. Nothing has really happened since except a lessening of interest until it was revived by the pollution crisis.

More recently, Lear Motors Corporation of Reno, Nevada, announced the development of a steam-powered engine for automobiles. This seems a bit like taking us back to the days of the Stanley Steamer, and many engineers don't believe there's a possible chance that a steam engine can be designed to meet the emission standards and yet offer the economy and performance that the American public demands. It would be simpler, they say, to modify the present internal combustion engine.

However, there are now two production cars that seem to have beat the pollution bugaboo. Both have unconventional power plants—one has a rotary engine like that of the Wankel offering, while the other is diesel-powered. Both—particularly the former, because of its price—are enjoying a pick-up in sales throughout the country, especially on the West Coast.

The car utilizing the Wankel rotary engine is the Mazda, a Japanese import that is also available with the internal combustion engine. Today's big selling point for the Mazda is that its rotary engine has combustion characteristics that hold the oxides of oxygen, toughest of all emissions to keep down, to a minimum, and that their imports all include a thermal reactor. This last, hung on the exhaust, is said to assure the Mazda's passing the tougher-than-tough '75 government standards.

The diesel-powered entry in this beat-the-pollution derby is the Mercedes-Benz 220D, which costs an arm and a leg in comparison to the Mazda. Like the Mazda, this German import is reputed to pass those 1975 standards right now, a questionable claim since there are no set routines for testing diesels for emissions.

The automobile industry felt the first full impact of gov-

149

ernment controls with the introduction of the 1973 models. The standards that had to be met covered more than just engine emissions. They included safety considerations designed to minimize damage from crashes.

All the '73s hit the road with the predicted lowering of performance and economy brought about because of the limitation on the amounts of nitrogen oxide emissions permitted. This meant less zip in the cars and less in miles per gallon of gas.

The safety standards for the 1973 cars brought about a return, somewhat in principle, to the old-style bumpers that used to stick out inches away from the car body. The regulations demanded bumpers that would protect a car in situations equivalent to a ten-mile-per-hour crash with another car, crashes that had been running up repair bills of $300 and more. The new bumpers took away some of the streamlining in styling, though some designs were less extreme than others.

General Motors kept the bumpers closer to the car body, using the type of shock absorber used on aircraft landing gears behind the bumpers so that on impact the bumper gives and then retracts. Ford utilized blocks of rubber in their energy-absorbing system, but with the bumpers extending out from the frame and body. Chrysler chose to design heavier bumpers and install large bumper guards.

Henry Ford II felt the public would be shocked when they saw the bumpers on the cars. "Some look like the cowcatchers that used to be on locomotives," he said. The big concern is the possible effect the new look will have on the car buyer who may not be happy with the cut-back in styling.

But what about the young American's love affair with muscle? Is the sporty car market completely closing down? Only time will answer that question. To judge from most of the automotive writers, while Mustang and Camaro are still alive and still outsell such sports imports as the Triumph, Jaguar, Datsun and Mercedes, their sales seem to have dropped as those of the imports rise. Where once newspaper ink flowed freely for pictures of Road Runner, Firebird, Mustang, Camaro and Javelin, the big attention getters today are the luxurious sporty types.

Cars like Ford's lush Continental Mark IV get the big stories. And then there's the other $10,000 job from Ford's Lincoln-Mercury Division, the Pantera, which some writers have called "the last of the red-hot supercars." Pantera may turn out to be a latter-day Edsel for Ford, another white elephant. But perhaps not, since it is an elegant and "different" sporty model. Yet the suspicions are there, perhaps because of the strange way in which Pantera joined the Ford stable.

Back around the middle 1960s, as the story goes, Henry

Chrysler-Plymouth

Road Runner's "Tomorrow Look" IF

MAG WHEELS AND RACING STRIPES

Ford tried to buy out the Ferraris in Italy, his eye on the continental look. As it turned out, Enzo Ferrari, the big name in European racing, wouldn't sell. And, the story goes on, Ford then sought out Alejandro de Tomaso, an Argentinian transplanted in Italy, who had designed a luxury car named Pantera ("Panther"). The deal was made. De Tomaso agreed to build Pantera for Ford.

Pantera is indeed different. Its engine, unlike that in most American cars, is not in front. Nor is it in back as in Volkswagen or the now dead Corvair. The Pantera engine is almost square in the middle. And its engine is not an Italian power plant, but the Ford 351-cubic-inch V-8. You'd find the identical engine powering many a Mustang, Cougar or Torino. If it weren't for that American 351, who knows how much more than $10,000 the car would cost?

But that gets us away from the main point, which is that hardly anyone can guess what will happen to muscle and performance come tomorrow, the day after or even five years from now, for that matter. The one thing you can depend on, at least to a point, is that a sporty-looking car, something different and personal, will always be the dream of a big chunk of the American car market, and the American automobile industry will come up with some way to give its public what it wants.

As the 1973s got ready for the market place it seemed almost certain that all of the industry had pulled in its horns and moved out of the performance field without fanfare owing to the federal emissions regulations. When the '73s were announced, there was Ford with at least one foot in the water.

Ford engineers had been able to make sufficient changes

DiTomaso Pantera

Ford Motor Company

in its 351-cubic-inch engine to satisfy the government standards and yet retain some high-performance capabilities. The 351, with its compression ratio reduced to 8.5 to 1, loses some horsepower and will not be able to match its previous elapsed time mark for the quarter mile; but it is still high-performance.

It is not available for all Ford cars, but for only one. This special version of the 351 (there are others) is the power plant for one, and only one, Mustang model dubbed the 351 HO or Boss 351 Mustang, first offered for 1973. It has few exterior changes and retains the pure Mustang look. On the road, with all the emission controls operative and using low-lead gas with a 91-octane rating, it will generate 275 horsepower at 6,000 rpm.

So Mustang, which marked the birth of the modern zoomies, may also be the last on the muscle scene. But don't bet on it.

Still, for the immediate future, there may not be a super-car to buy. Very likely the one with the most muscle won't be a long-hooded and low-slung hot super beast, growling in the night and belching flames and smoke through double exhausts.

The 351 HO gives us hope, however. The chances are that we'll still have a good performer, long-hooded and low-slung. But the menacing roar and the blasting take-off won't be there.

GLOSSARY OF MUSCLE CAR TERMS

ALL OUT—   Maximum speed; a full-scale competition car.

BIG ARM—   Long piston stroke.

BIG BORE—   Engine with larger than normal bore (cylinder diameters).

BITE—   Traction on a race track.

BLOW OFF—   Pass a car as if it's standing still.

BOMB—   A car of exceptional performance.

BOOTS—   Tires.

BOTTOM GEAR—   Lowest driving gear.

BOX—   Transmission.

BOTTOM OUT—   Centrifugal force on a car as it enters a high-bank turn on a high-speed run.

BUG CATCHER—   The scoop or hood around the injector system on a supercharged engine.

BUMP STICK—   Camshaft.

CALIFORNIA RAKE— Hot rod and custom car alteration where the front axle is lowered and larger rear tires are installed, raising the rear.

CC— Abbreviation for cubic centimeter; the European measurement that is the basis for engine displacement. (1,000 cc = 1 liter = 62 cubic inches. 1 American cubic inch = 16.38 cc.)

CHEATERS— Slick tread rear tires used in competition events.

CHRISTMAS TREE— Set of colored lights on a short pole used to start races, especially drags.

CHROMIES— Simulated magnesium racing wheels (mag wheels) or chrome wheels used to dress up a car.

CLUNKER— A sluggish, beat-up car.

CRANK— The crankshaft.

CUBES— Cubic inch displacement in an engine.

DIG OUT— Accelerate rapidly from a standing start.

DOWNSHIFT— Descend through gears from a higher to lower.

DRAG STRIP— Quarter-mile race course with deceleration area. Also, any paved stretch used for straight-line acceleration tests.

DUAL QUAD— Carburetor installation using two carburetors, each with four throats.

ELIMINATOR— A drag car that wins by eliminating other cars in its class by running at a lower elapsed time.

E. T.— Abbreviation for "elapsed time" used in drag racing, road races and rallies.

FASTBACK— A car with a sloping back.

F. I.— Abbreviation for fuel injection, a system by which fuel is sprayed directly into engine cylinders rather than through a carburetor.

FISHTAIL— Lateral sway in the rear of a car when racing. Also to drive in such a manner.

FLAT OUT— Driving at top speed.

FOUR-SPEED— Abbreviation for four-speed manual transmission. Also referred to as "four-on-the-floor."

FOUR BARREL— A four-venturi (throat or opening) carburetor.

FULL HOUSE— A car (or engine) with every possible performance modification short of supercharging.

GINGERBREAD— Slang for chrome ornamentation on a car.

GO BUTTON— Slang for the accelerator pedal.

COOK WAGON— Hot-rod description for an over-chromed stock car with no performance refinements.

GT— Abbreviation for Gran Turismo, a car usually equipped for two people and luggage and equally applicable to fast over-the-road touring or class racing.

GYMKHANA— A competitive event to test driving powers consisting of timed contests in backing, parking and avoiding obstacles, also called a Road-E-O.

HAIRY—   A car that is a hot performer.

HEMI—   Abbreviation for a competition engine with hemispheric combustion chambers.

HONKER—   Drag term for a hot performing car. A winner.

HOT DOG—   Leading driver on a racing circuit.

IRON—   Slang for family-type cars, any models not sports or high-performance.

JUG—   Slang for carburetor.

KNOCK-OFF—   A quickly removable wheel lug.

LEADFOOT—   A fast driver.

MAGS—   Magnesium or aluminum wheels available in dealerships or hot-rod shops.

MILL—   Slang for the engine.

MOON GAS—   Slang term for fuels with high nitromethane content.

OFF THE PEG—   Sports car term for pushing an engine's rpms beyond the upper limit of the tachometer.

PEAKING SPEED—   Engine rpm at which peak performance is attained.

PEEL—   Accelerate so that rear tires deposit rubber on the road. Also referred to as "burning rubber."

RAG TOP—   A convertible.

RAIL JOB—   A dragster with little or no body and exposed frame rails.

SANITARY—   Slang for a car of unusual cleanliness

despite competition potential. Also a car unusually well prepared for competition.

SCOOP— Opening in the body to deliver cool air to the engine, brakes or cockpit.

SCREAMER— A high-rpm engine. A fast or supercharged car.

SLEEPER— A racing car that performs better than expected.

SLICK— Smooth, treadless racing or drag tire of wide cross-section.

STANDING QUARTER—In drag racing, a quarter-mile time race begun with the vehicle at rest.

SUPER STOCK— A production car with special engine and chassis modifications.

THROAT— A carburetor venturi (opening).

TOP END— Power output at high rpm or at the end of a quarter mile.

WHEELIE— Picking up the front wheels off the ground when coming off the line.

ABOUT THE AUTHOR

David J. Abodaher was born in Streator, Illinois, but moved with his family at the age of five to Detroit, Michigan, where he has lived most of his life. He attended Detroit parochial schools, with his college years spent at the University of Detroit and Notre Dame, paying his own way through free-lance writing.

His first efforts, written and sold in his late teens, were mystery, western and sports pulp fiction, followed by radio dramas. Leaving Notre Dame after the first semester of his senior year, he entered the broadcasting field full time, writing dramatic scripts and documentaries and announcing sports. He also worked as producer and program director at radio stations in Detroit, Cincinnati, Oklahoma City and Kalamazoo.

During World War II he served in the U.S. Army Signal Corps and when the war was over, he returned to Detroit and entered the field of advertising. Appointed Radio Director of his agency, he found himself back in the broadcast area, writing commercial spots and doing on-the-air assignments in sports.

Moving into business for himself as a creator and producer of radio and television features, he also put his interest and knowledge of photography to work, writing, directing and producing commercial and public-service motion pictures. Special writing and photography assignments for the Ford Motor Company led him back into advertising with the Ford agency, the J. Walter Thompson Company, and then to Kenyon & Eckhardt, Inc. He is currently Senior Writer for A. R. Brasch, Inc., involved with sales promotion and training programs for Ford, GM and Chrysler.

Mr. Abodaher is an American history buff and the author of several biographies for young people. His hobby, other than photography, is reading history. He has one daughter, Lynda.